Introduction

Reading Section

Writing Section

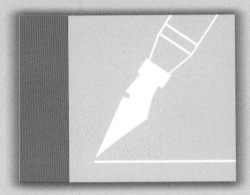

Reading Section

Writing Section

Aiming for A* is a new concept in revision guides. The objective of most revision guides is simply to help you pass your exam by providing revision notes on all the material that could come up… the rest is up to you. However, if you are not content just to pass – you really want to excel and achieve the highest marks possible – Aiming for A* is for you.

This guide provides full coverage of all the externally assessed material on GCSE AQA English Specification A. It also provides invaluable advice and guidance on how to boost your grades and work towards getting top marks in the exams.

On this course, you will sit two exam papers (on different days); each paper has two sections. This book is divided up in exactly the same way so that you can prepare for each paper / section separately.

Each section in the guide begins by clarifying the nature of that part of the exam: the skills being assessed, the time allowed to answer each question, the number of questions that must be answered, and what the examiners will be looking for in your answers.

This guide focuses on the reading and writing skills expected from an A* candidate to ensure that you know exactly what is required to achieve the top mark, with regard to your use of language, vocabulary and grammar, the features that you should be able to identify in a variety of pieces of writing, and your ability to use a range of appropriate writing styles and structures to produce sophisticated answers.

Featuring questions that reflect those on the Higher Tier papers, the guide includes tasks and activities which provide excellent exam preparation and help you to hone your advanced skills, along with hints and tips to help you reach your A* potential.

Additional helpful information is given, including useful language terms, and common punctuation, grammar and spelling errors, to provide a useful reference when studying for either paper.

Aiming for A* in GCSE AQA English is written by an expert team of English teachers / examiners with over 40 years' teaching experience between them: Paul Burns, Jan Edge and Philippa Ronan.

Their experience as GCSE examiners means that they have an excellent understanding of the criteria used for marking English papers and are able to offer invaluable advice on how to achieve an A* in GCSE English.

Contents

4 Common Errors:
Punctuation, Grammar and Spelling
6 Language Terms
8 Exam Overview

Paper 1 Section A

10 Reading Non-fiction and Media Texts
11 What are Non-fiction and Media Texts?
12 Non-fiction and Media Questions
13 Writing Your Answer
14 Non-fiction and Media Terms
15 Purpose, Audience, Form and Language
16 Techniques in Non-fiction and Media Texts
19 Recognising Fact and Opinion
20 Analysing Language and Structure
22 Analysing Presentation
23 Developing Your Answer
27 Exam Practice and Exam Tips

Paper 1 Section B

28 Writing to Argue, Persuade or Advise
30 Purpose, Audience, Form and Language
32 Planning Your Answer
33 Structure: Sentences
34 Structure: Paragraphs
35 Language
37 Form
40 Writing to Argue
42 Writing to Persuade
44 Writing to Advise
46 Exam Tips

Paper 2 Section A

48 Reading Poetry from Different Cultures
49 Culture and Traditions
50 Poetry Terms
51 Limbo
52 Nothing's Changed
53 Island Man
54 Blessing
55 Two Scavengers in a Truck…
56 Night of the Scorpion
57 Vultures
58 What Were They Like?
59 (From) Search for My Tongue
60 (From) Unrelated Incidents
61 Half-Caste
62 Love After Love

63 This Room
64 Not My Business
65 Presents from My Aunts…
66 Hurricane Hits England
67 Comparing Poems
69 Exam Tips and Exam Practice
70 Developing Your Answer

Paper 2 Section B

72 Writing to Inform, Explain or Describe
Writing to Inform or Explain (pages 74–85)
74 Purpose, Audience, Form and Language
76 Planning Your Answer
77 Structure: Sentences
79 Language: Humour and Irony
80 Form
83 Personal and Impersonal Writing
84 Writing to Inform or Explain
Writing to Describe (pages 86–93)
86 Purpose, Audience and Form
88 Planning Your Answer
90 Choosing Your Subject
92 Writing to Describe
94 Exam Tips

95 Index

Common Errors

Punctuation

Punctuation and grammar are very important in order to convey meaning through a piece of writing. You will be expected to use punctuation and grammar correctly in the exam. Here are some of the most common errors that students make. Some may seem simple, but it is amazing how many able students make them. Such errors can give a very bad impression to the examiner. Read the information and make sure you understand it.

Full Stops (.)

Full stops separate sentences. Without them, writing does not make sense.

Commas (,)

Commas are used to mark smaller breaks or pauses than full stops. They must not be used to link two separate statements which could stand alone as sentences, unless a word like 'who', 'which' or 'that' is used, for example…
- I fed the dog, which was hungry.   ✓
- I fed the dog, it was hungry.   ✗

Commas are used to separate subordinate clauses from main clauses. Subordinate clauses give additional information but are not necessary for the sentence to make sense, for example…
- Amy , having eaten ten bananas, was feeling sick.
- Tom , the football captain, scored two goals.

The coloured phrases could be taken out and the sentences would still make sense.

Commas are used to list items, for example…
- He bought sugar, butter, eggs and flour.

Commas are also used to introduce speech, for example…
- He replied hurriedly, 'I'm going!'

Question Marks (?)

Question marks come at the end of questions. They are used in direct speech, but not in indirect (reported) speech, for example…
- 'Did you see Lizzie at the party?' asked Ben.   ✓
- Ben asked me if I'd seen Lizzie at the party?   ✗

Dashes (–)

A pair of dashes can be used instead of brackets and placed around an extra idea which has been inserted into a sentence, for example…
- I went into the restaurant – if you could call it that – and ordered a drink.

Ellipsis (…)

Ellipsis can indicate a thought that trails off. It is used in writing to create a sense of foreboding or anticipation, for example…
- I wasn't the only one in there…

Colons (:)

Colons are used before an explanation or example, for example…
- The marathon was a very long race: 26 miles!

Colons also appear before a list, for example…
- The house was surrounded by flowers: blue azaleas, red poppies, lilies and roses.

The part before the colon must be a clause (a phrase that could act as a complete sentence), but the part after it does not need to be.

Semi-colons (;)

Semi-colons are used to show that two sentences are closely related, for example…
- It may be cancelled; it depends on the weather.

The parts before and after the semi-colon must be clauses. They also separate words or phrases in a list.

Apostrophes (')

Apostrophes are used to show omission or contraction (usually in speech or in informal writing). The apostrophe replaces the missing letter(s), for example…
- He shouldn't have gone. (Should not = shouldn't)
- You'll never understand. (You will = you'll)
- Mark's finished his work but Rachel's still doing hers. (Mark has = Mark's, Rachel is = Rachel's)

Apostrophes are also used to show possession (ownership). If the owner is singular, or the word for plural owners does not end in 's' (e.g. sheep, men, children), add an apostrophe and an 's' to the word that indicates the owner, for example…
- The cat's tail (i.e. the tail of the cat – one cat).
- The boy's shoes (i.e. the shoes of the boy – one boy).
- The children's books (i.e. the books of the children – more than one child).

If there is more than one owner and the word indicating the owners ends in 's', simply add an apostrophe at the end, for example…
- The cats' tails (i.e. the tails of the cats – more than one cat).
- The boys' shoes (i.e. the shoes of the boys – more than one boy).

Grammar

Done / did, and seen / saw

These words are often used incorrectly.
- I did it   I saw it   ✓
- I have done it   I have seen it   ✓
- I done it   I seen it   ✗

Could, would, should, ought to, might, may, must, can, will, shall

These are modal verbs. They are never followed by 'of'. They are followed by 'have', for example…
- I could have won the race.   ✓
- I could of won the race.   ✗

I / me

'I' is the subject of a sentence; 'me' is the object. For example…
- Lucy and I went to the cinema.   ✓
- Me and Lucy went to the cinema.   ✗
- She left champagne for Tony and me.   ✓
- She left champagne for Tony and I.   ✗

Spelling

Accept	– to receive: 'I accept your gift'.
Except	– without: 'all the boys except John went'.
Aloud	– out loud: 'read your work aloud'.
Allowed	– permitted: 'chewing is not allowed in the classroom'.
Hear	– to hear with your ears: 'I can hear music'.
Here	– in this place: 'It's over here'.
Its	– belonging to it: 'the cat licked its paws'.
It's	– short for 'it is': 'it's a long way home'.
Lay / lie	– The past tense of 'lie' is' lay': 'last night I lay on my bed for a while'.
	– In the present tense you 'lay a table' or, if you are a hen, 'lay an egg'.
No	– opposite of 'yes': 'no, I didn't like it'.
New	– opposite of old: 'it's a new bag'.
Know / knew	– aware: 'I didn't know he knew about it'.
Passed	– a verb: 'I passed all my GCSEs'.
Past	– a noun indicating a previous time: 'it's all in the past now'. (Also used in phrases such as 'he went past' or 'they are past their best'.)

Practice	– a noun: 'netball practice is cancelled'.
Practise	– a verb: 'you must practise every day'. (The same rule applies to advice / advise.)
Quite	– fairly, a bit: 'the essay was quite good'.
Quiet	– silent: 'the class was quiet'.
Right	– opposite of wrong: 'that is right!'.
Write	– what you do in an exam. Someone who writes is a writer: 'she writes well'.
There	– in that place: 'I'll be there soon'. (Also used in phrases such as 'there is', 'there are' etc.)
They're	– 'they are': 'they're not friends'.
Their	– belonging to them: 'they left their bags'.
To	– towards: 'he went to bed'. (Also part of the infinitive of a verb, 'to do', 'to think' etc.)
Too	– excessively: 'we had too many sweets'.
Two	– the number 2: 'there were two bears'.
Where	– a place: 'where did you say it was?'.
We're	– 'we are': 'we're not sure'.
Wear	– used with clothes etc.: 'I will wear my gold earrings'.
Were	– part of the verb 'to be': 'they were not very happy'.
Whether	– if: 'I don't know whether to go or not'.
Weather	– the sun, rain etc.: 'the weather was good'.
Whose	– belonging to whom: 'whose coat is it?'.
Who's	– 'who is' / 'who has': 'who's that boy?' 'who's dropped that coat?'.

Language Terms

The following language terms are used in all kinds of writing. You will have used these terms in class (especially when discussing poetry) to describe the techniques that writers use in their work. The following list is a reminder of the main techniques and why a writer might use them. The terms are mentioned throughout the revision guide, so it will help you to read through them before you start to revise.

Accent: the way a character would sound if they were speaking, e.g. a cockney accent is used by most of the characters in *Eastenders*. Accent can be conveyed through the use of non-standard spelling, e.g. 'ah wunder'd where tha'd bin' to portray a Yorkshire accent. *Used to show where a character is from and to indicate something about his / her way of life.*

Alliteration: repetition of a sound at the beginning of words, e.g. 'big balls bounced'. *Used to stress certain words or phrases.*

Ambiguity: a sentence or word can have more than one meaning (it is ambiguous), e.g. 'Mary had a little lamb'. This could mean Mary kept a small lamb, or Mary ate a bit of lamb. *Used to express more than one meaning at once, and to make the audience think.*

Assonance: rhyme of the internal vowel sound, e.g. 'jump and push', 'cat in the bag'. *Used to slow the reader down and to emphasise certain words.*

Connotation: the meaning that is suggested by the use of a particular word, e.g. red could indicate danger. *Used to make a point in a subtle way.*

Contrast: a strong difference between two things. *Often used to highlight political issues.*

Dialect: the words and grammar that speakers use. Regional dialects differ from the Standard English dialect. Each dialect has its own special words and ways of using grammar. *Used to show which social group a character belongs to. A writer might give characters different dialects to show that they are from different social groups, and to create a sharper contrast.*

Elision: running a word into others, e.g. 'fish 'n' chips'. *Used to suggest spontaneous speech and informal language.*

Enjambment: when lines run on and are not stopped at the end. *Often used in poetry to create a free-flowing effect.*

Exclamations: show anger, shock, horror, surprise and joy, e.g. 'I won!'. *Used to portray emotions.*

Imagery: the use of descriptive words which allow you to create a picture in your mind. *Used to involve the reader in the moment being described.*

Irony and sarcasm: the use of words to imply the opposite of their meaning. *Used to make fun of people or issues. For example, if your friend had chicken pox and you said to him / her 'Your skin looks nice today', you would be using sarcasm.*

Juxtaposition: the positioning of two words, phrases or ideas next to or near each other. *Used to highlight a contrast between the two words, phrases or ideas.*

Lineation: arrangement in lines that are stopped at the end. *Used to present separate ideas and to create a sense of the lines / ideas being disjointed and erratic.*

Metaphor: an image created by referring to something as something else, e.g. 'the army of ants was on the rampage'. Here the ants are referred to as an army. *Used to give additional information to the reader to create a particular effect or to emphasise a point.*

Onomatopoeia: a word that sounds like what it describes, e.g. 'splash', 'boom'. *Used to appeal to the senses of the reader, in this case their hearing.*

Oxymoron: two contradictory terms placed together, e.g. 'bitter sweet', 'cruel kindness'. *Used to make each term stand out and to highlight a contrast.*

Pathetic fallacy: when the surroundings (e.g. the weather) reflect the mood of the character. *Used to create mood in the writing.*

Personification: making an object sound like a person, giving it human qualities, e.g. 'the fingers of the tree grabbed at my hair as I passed'. *Used to enable the reader to identify with what is being personified and helps to create a specific image.*

Puns (also referred to as **play on words**): words used in an amusing way to suggest other meanings, e.g. 'she's parking mad!'. *Used to entertain and amuse, and to imply another meaning.*

Questions (interrogatives): show that the writer wants the reader to consider the question, or that they themselves are considering the question asked. *Used to show a range of things about a character such as inquisitiveness, upset and confusion.*

Received Pronunciation: the accent used by many national newsreaders. You cannot tell which part of the country a Received Pronunciation speaker comes from. This accent is seen as prestigious (impressive) and is associated with social groups that are well-educated and wealthy.

Repetition: when words, phrases, sentences or structures are repeated. *Used to stress certain words or key points in the piece of writing.*

Rhetorical questions: for example, when your teachers ask 'do you think that is funny?' they do not expect you to answer. Such questions do not require an answer; the answer is obvious. *Used to make you think about the question that has been asked.*

Rhyme: the use of rhyming words which affects the sound patterns. Sound patterns can be regular or irregular. *The rhyme can adjust the tone of a poem, or can emphasise a point such as in newspaper headlines.*

Rhythm: the beat of the writing (mainly poems) when read aloud: fast or slow, regular or irregular. *The rhythm of the writing (poetry) can add to its overall effect.*

Sibilance: alliteration with the 's' sound, e.g. 'the silent stranger slipped away'. *Used to stress certain words or phrases or to create tone, e.g. a sinister tone.*

Simile: a comparison of one thing to another that includes the words 'as' or 'like', e.g. 'the man was as cold as ice', 'the pain was like a searing heat passing through her'. *Used to give additional information to the reader to create a particular effect or to emphasise a point.*

Standard English: the conventional use of words and grammar in the English language.

Superlatives: words which express the best or worst of something. They often end in 'est' or have 'most' or 'least' before them, e.g. 'highest', 'happiest', 'most beautiful', 'least stylish'. *Used to emphasise a point.*

Symbols and symbolism: a symbol is an object which represents an abstract idea, e.g. a dove symbolises peace, red symbolises danger. *Used to create a stronger, more vivid image.*

Synonyms: words with similar meanings, e.g. hole, pit, ditch. *Used to provide linguistic variation in a piece of writing.*

Tone: the overall attitude of the writing, e.g. formal, informal, playful, angry, suspicious, ironic. *Used to allow the emotions of the writer (or the character in the writing) to be expressed.*

Exam Overview

The Paper

The Higher Tier GCSE AQA English exam consists of two papers which the students sit on separate days. Each paper is divided into two sections: reading skills and writing skills.

Paper	Section	Section Title	Questions	Time Allowed
1	A	Reading Non-fiction and Media Texts	Answer all questions	1 hour
1	B	Writing to Argue, Persuade or Advise	Answer one question	45 minutes
2	A	Reading Poetry from Different Cultures	Answer one question	45 minutes
2	B	Writing to Inform, Explain or Describe	Answer one question	45 minutes

The Questions

Read the exam paper and each question very carefully. Look out for small words in the questions such as 'and' and 'or'. Make sure you understand exactly what the question is asking you to do before you begin to answer it.

You must make it very clear which question you are answering in the exam. Give the number of the question you have chosen to answer. In Paper 1 Section A, where you must answer all the questions, make it obvious where one answer finishes and the next one begins. Do not let one answer run into another.

The Importance of Planning and Checking

In each section of the exam, you should spend about five minutes at the beginning planning your answer, and five minutes at the end checking your answer.

It is very important and very beneficial to plan your answer. Examiners like to see that you have planned your work. A plan reminds you to structure your work in paragraphs, and helps to produce a good answer which is clear, logical and flows well.

It is equally as important to check your work. Read it through and ensure you have covered everything you wanted to. Make sure that the words you have chosen put across the exact idea or effect that you

intended them to. Check your spelling and punctuation – it is easy to make mistakes when you are under pressure.

Tips to Help You Prepare for the English Exam

- Identify errors that you frequently make and practise until you are no longer making them. Use the information on pages 4–5 to help you.
- Learn the terms for the language techniques listed on pages 6–7 – what they describe, why they are used, and how the terms are spelt.
- Work through the Exam Preparation and Exam Practice tasks in this guide.
- Try writing answers to the example questions that are given throughout the book, within the time allowed in the actual exam.
- Read over some of the work you have done in school (especially work done under exam conditions) and think about how it could be improved.

Remember that the information in this revision guide is not intended to replace what you have learned in class, just to provide you with key points to help with your revision.

Try to stay calm in the exam and enjoy writing your answers. Make the most of the chance to express yourself.

Paper 1

Section A

10   Reading Non-fiction and Media Texts

Section B

28   Writing to Argue, Persuade or Advise

Reading Non-fiction and Media Texts

The Exam Questions

In Section A of Paper 1 you will be tested on your reading response to non-fiction / media texts. You will be provided with two theme-related non-fiction / media texts on a loose insert inside the exam paper, on which you will be asked two questions. Each question will tell you how many marks it is worth in brackets, which will give you an idea of how much you are expected to write. You must answer **all** the questions and all the parts to the questions. It is recommended that you spend about one hour on this section of the paper.

What is the examiner looking for?

The examiner wants to see that you can read, understand and interpret non-fiction and media texts. It is important that you present your answers clearly and logically.

In order to obtain a grade A or A*, your responses to the texts must show that you can do the following.

- Understand the writers' ideas and attitudes.
- Identify and analyse argument, opinion and alternative interpretations of the texts.
- Discuss and develop your interpretations of the texts.
- Explain the obvious 'surface' meaning and also try to read 'between the lines' for a meaning on a deeper level.

- Make a personal response to the texts.
- Distinguish between fact and opinion.
- Follow an argument by identifying implications and recognising inconsistencies.
- Make apt and careful comparisons within and between the texts.
- Pick out details from the texts effectively, using references and quotations to back up the points you make.
- Recognise and understand linguistic features such as irony and sarcasm (see page 79).
- Understand and evaluate how linguistic, structural and presentational devices are used for effect.
- Comment on how the language varies and changes.
- Consider the effects of the writers' use of language and the way they create mood, atmosphere etc.

Examiner's Tips

Highlight the key terms in the question to ensure that you answer the question that has been asked. If you have time, write these terms down the side of the texts to ensure that you refer to them.

Read the texts at least twice before attempting your answer. You often see things during the second reading that you had not noticed the first time – especially subtle, stylistic devices such as irony, sarcasm and humour.

Many thanks to Oxfam for use of material: © Oxfam GB Reproduced by permission.

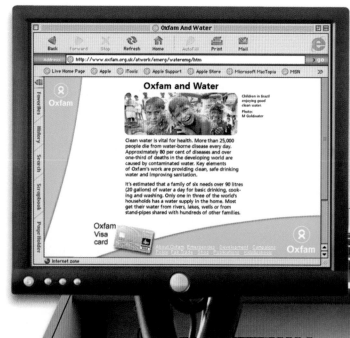

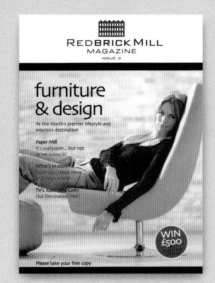

Non-fiction Texts

A non-fiction text refers to any text that is factual and aims to give you information in some way. They are written to inform, explain, persuade, advise, argue or describe. Their form and presentation usually help to relay the information. Non-fiction covers many types of texts, including all media texts. Examples include...

- hard-hitting articles stating opinions
- travel books
- diaries or journals written by real people
- lists of instructions
- dictionary definitions or encyclopaedia entries
- biographies (accounts of people's lives, written by someone else) and autobiographies (accounts of people's lives, written by themselves)
- documentary scripts
- information sheets
- web pages for various charities and appeals.

You may get any of the texts listed above in your exam. However, there are many more texts which come under 'non-fiction'; non-fiction texts can include anything which is not a poem, story, novel or play.

Exam Preparation

1. Try regularly reading some non-fiction texts. Try to work out which techniques the writers use to get their information across.
2. Choose an article from a magazine. Underline all the interesting stylistic features you can find. Ask yourself what you think the writer's opinions are about the topic and how these are conveyed.

Media Texts

The term 'media text' refers to a text that expresses fact, or expresses opinion in a factual way (see page 19). Media covers many types of texts and includes...

- newspaper articles, reports, features, editorials or letters
- magazine articles, reports, features or letters
- images and cartoons with captions
- pamphlets and leaflets
- brochures
- advertisements
- promotional material / literature
- web pages.

Media texts may inform, describe, argue a case, advise, explain, or simply entertain. A large proportion of media texts, however, try to persuade you to do something such as donate money to a charity, buy a product, or agree with a particular point of view. For example, newspapers often want their readers to agree with their opinions. You need to think about the techniques used to assist in persuading the reader.

Exam Preparation

1. Find two different texts that cover the same topic. Compare their effectiveness. Decide which text is the most effective in achieving its purpose and explain why. Aim to write at least two sides of A4.
2. Read a broadsheet newspaper weekly and cut out any interesting articles that you find. Apply questions from this section of the revision guide (such as the one above) to them.

Non-fiction and Media Questions

Many thanks to DEFRA for permission to use this leaflet.

In the exam you will be asked to write about…

- the purpose of the text – to inform, instruct, persuade, entertain etc.
- the use of language to shape the reader's response
- the writers' views and opinions
- the use of fact and opinion
- presentational devices and form.

The texts that you are given to analyse will contain pictures, photographs or other presentational features. You will be asked to comment on the presentational features of the texts in conjunction with the stylistic (language) features.

There is usually one question which asks you to compare the texts; this means that you must write about the texts equally, drawing attention to similarities and differences between them, and making cross-references where appropriate.

Key Words in a Question

The following key words tell you straightaway what the question is asking you to do. Underline the key words in each question to ensure that you answer the question asked – a prerequisite for gaining a top grade.

What	– describe something.
Why	– explain something.
How	– identify the writer's techniques.
Discuss	– suggest different meanings / viewpoints.

Comment	– analyse something and read 'between the lines'.
Compare	– study both texts for similarities and differences.
Explain	– show through reference to the texts.
Form and presentation	– how the texts are structured and how they appear on the page.
Reader's response	– how the writer intends the reader to react to the article.

Exam Preparation

Highlight the key words in these questions.

- Comment on how the writer uses facts and opinions to support the points he is making.
- Discuss the ways in which language is used in the article to shape the reader's response.

Choose an article from a broadsheet newspaper that interests you and apply question 2 (above) to it. Aim to write two sides of A4, as a minimum, within one hour.

Examiner's Tip

Read the questions before you read the texts. The questions will tell you exactly what to look out for and will enable you to focus your reading on the information you need for your answers.

Writing Your Answer

Remember that you have only one hour in which to plan and write your answer. It needs to be written in a way befitting an A / A* candidate. Your responses should be well-planned, well-structured and expressed using impressive and sophisticated vocabulary.

In order to obtain a high grade you must show that you are a discerning reader and can pick out aspects of the style of the texts that other, less perceptive readers might not have noticed.

It is important to learn how to extract information from texts quickly and efficiently.

- Read the questions so that you know what to highlight in the texts as you read them through a second or third time.
- Read through both texts and try to work out the main points of each.
- Re-read the texts to look for the information requested in the questions. This is called scanning.
- Underline the key points / pieces of information.
- Think about the style, layout, presentational devices and tone of the texts.
- Spend about one quarter of your time reading the texts and planning your answers.

The PEE Technique

Always use the 'PEE' technique in your answers. You may have referred to this as '123' or as another term which indicates that you must have a three part response to your answers:

P Make a **P**oint
E Use **E**vidence from the text (a quote or example)
E Give an **E**xplanation to back up the point. Explain why the evidence illustrates your point.

Your explanation section will be the one to help determine whether or not you deserve the highest grade, so write in detail.

When writing your answer...
- begin confidently. Your first sentence should show that you know exactly what the question is asking
- make sure that every sentence you write is relevant to the question and make sure you are concise
- use the correct technical terms
- try to use impersonal language like 'It seems' or 'It appears' rather than 'I think' – this will make you sound sure of yourself
- be analytical: suggest why certain words or images have been used and comment on their effect
- use examples and quotes from the text and layout to consolidate your points

Examiner's Tips

Spend some time reading the texts, underlining key points and making brief notes in the margins.

You must apply the technical terminology to the texts, use the PEE technique and make concise and perceptive comments about the texts, making cross-references where appropriate.

Non-fiction and Media Terms

You should always use the correct technical terms when referring to, commenting upon and analysing non-fiction and media texts.

Broadsheet – A large-sized newspaper (e.g. *The Telegraph*), which reports news in detail and has a formal register. Many broadsheets now come as smaller, 'compact' newspapers.

Tabloid – A small-sized newspaper (e.g. *The Sun*), which contains news, gossip and celebrity stories, and is written in a more colloquial register.

Headline – The title of a main article.

Strapline – An introductory headline just below a main headline.

By-line – The reporter's name, usually given under the headline.

Sub-headings – Headings used to break up the text.

Cross-heads – Sub-headings which appear within a block of text; these are often quotes.

Lead story – The main story on the front page of a newspaper or magazine.

Feature article – An article which covers a topic in some depth and is not usually about current news.

Human interest story – An article that focuses on a personal story, which is often sentimental.

Editorial – An opinion column which gives the newspaper's (or editor's) point of view.

Columns – The layout of articles in newspapers and magazines.

Caption – A few words or a short sentence which explains what a photo or picture illustrates.

Slogan – A catchy, memorable phrase often used in advertising.

Logo – A symbol or emblem unique to a product or company, used to represent that product or company.

Text box – A box containing text.

Font size – The size of the text.

Italic – A sloping font style: *italic*.

Font type – The type of font used (e.g. Comic Sans, Times New Roman, Arial).

Purpose, Audience, Form and Language

When producing a piece of non-fiction or media writing, the writer considers the following:

- **Purpose:** why the piece is being written – to inform, instruct, question, analyse, persuade etc.
- **Audience:** who it is being written for – adults, teenagers, children, men, women, teachers etc.
- **Language:** how it is being written – style and tone.
- **Form and presentation:** how it is being presented – article, advert etc., and images, font size etc.

Purpose and Audience

The purpose of the text and its intended audience have a direct relation to the style in which it is written and the language devices that the writer employs.

Firstly, you need to work out what the text is trying to achieve and the audience at which it is aimed.

- **Does it contain argument, persuasive devices, opinions or facts?** Is the purpose of this to inform, persuade, or change the reader's opinion?
- **Does it contain descriptions of people, places or emotions?** Is the purpose of this to move the reader, recreate the past, gain the reader's sympathy etc.?
- **Is it a narrative account (told as a sequence of events)?** Is the purpose of this to entertain, engage, shock or motivate the reader?
- **Is the register formal or informal?** Is this to target a young or old audience?
- **Is the tone masculine or feminine (i.e. vocabulary aimed specifically at men or women)?** Is this to target a male or female audience?
- **Does it contain jargon?** Is this to target a specific group of people (e.g. legal jargon aimed at people working in the legal profession?

Form

Form refers to the way in which a text is presented. A text could be in the form of a letter, leaflet, article in a newspaper or magazine, web page etc. The form can affect the language and style used in a piece of writing, for example, a newspaper headline might use alliteration or puns. The form also determines the extent of the presentational devices used in a text.

Language

The diction and stylistic devices employed by the writer are dependent upon audience and purpose. To gain an A* the examiner wants to see that you can identify and comment upon these features in a concise, exploratory and incisive way, making cross-references where appropriate.

Style refers to the overall effect created by the language (and presentational devices) used and its intended effect on the reader.

The language may be simple, using uncomplicated vocabulary and short sentences; it may be highly descriptive, using lots of adverbs and adjectives; it may be formal, using Standard English and an impersonal tone; it may be informal, using slang, contractions and a structure that reflects spoken English, etc.

You must be able to identify and comment on all the stylistic features covered in this guide.

Tone refers to the mood, feeling or atmosphere created in a text. For example, speeches by politicians have a passionate, personal tone to emphasise that the speaker believes in what he / she is expounding, whilst an article in a professional journal would probably have an impersonal, academic tone to sound informative and well-researched.

The tone of a non-fiction or media text could be amusing / humorous, sarcastic, critical, passionate, rebellious, serious, morose etc. The language is used in a way that influences how the readers feel about the characters, ideas and events in a text.

Techniques in Non-fiction and Media Texts

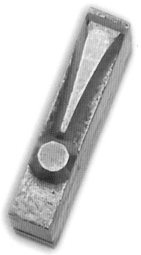

Language Techniques

Media texts often have a persuasive tone. Other texts may have a tone that is informative, argumentative, light-hearted, lively, humourous, emotional etc.

Tone and mood are created through the use of various language techniques:

- **Narrative voice:** use of the first person (I, we, us, our etc.) gives an effect of the writer sharing an experience with the reader. This makes it sound more personal. A text may be written in the third person (he, she, it, they etc.) which gives a more impersonal tone, and is usually more formal.
- **Address:** writers often use the second person personal pronoun (you, your). This is known as the direct address pronoun. It adds a personal touch and engages the reader as it sounds friendly, inviting and even confiding. It is employed in persuasive writing to directly involve the reader in the issue being discussed.
- **Speech:** a piece of writing may contain direct speech (the exact words someone said, e.g. 'It was great'), indirect speech (e.g. she said it was great) or thoughts (when we hear someone's thoughts, e.g. she thought about how great it was). Thoughts are usually found in novels, diaries and autobiographies, which add to the overall personal tone. Direct speech and indirect speech are often used in newspaper and magazine articles, to add realism to the story and to make the reader identify with people in it, perhaps to gain sympathy.
- **Connotations:** hidden meanings and associations can be implied effectively through writing. Words may be used symbolically, as well as literally, to make the reader think.

- **Sensational and emotive language:** writers use language to be dramatic or to make the reader feel a particular emotion, e.g. excitement, anger or sympathy. Charity adverts are good examples of how writers try to manipulate the readers' response. They often use language to try to gain the readers' sympathy (and therefore persuade them to donate to the charity), for example…
  - Poor Scamp was found starving, shivering and shaking in a cardboard box. He is still small for his age and needs constant medical attention.
- **Exaggeration / hyperbole:** exaggeration (hyperbole) is used in persuasive or amusing writing to give greater emphasis. Exaggeration often includes **superlatives**, for example, when the piece of writing states that something is the best, the greatest, the cleanest, the most effective, the least attractive etc. Phrases from adverts are a good example of how writing uses exaggeration to grab the reader's attention. For example…
  - The cheapest prices in town!
- **Rhetorical questions:** rhetorical questions are used to make the reader consider what is being asked, and can be found in articles, promotional leaflets, and adverts, for example…
  - Thousands of cars are stolen every year. Is this kind of behaviour acceptable in our society?
- **Alliteration:** this is used in pieces of writing to make a group of words stand out or to make something memorable. It is a technique employed in newspaper headlines. For example…
  - House Prices Hit All Time High
- **Rule of three:** one of the easiest and most useful ways of emphasising a point is by using three words or phrases. This can be found in media texts such as newspaper articles, for example…
  - Restructuring the present system would be an expensive, time-consuming and unworkable nightmare.
- **Repetition:** sometimes a word or a group of words is repeated for emphasis. Repetition is used in advertising, in newspaper articles, and in promotional leaflets. For example…
  - Fact: more people than ever own credit cards. Fact: more people than ever are in debt.
- **Juxtaposition:** this creates a strong contrast by putting two ideas side by side. It highlights the difference between the two ideas, for example…
  - The Ethiopian baby is starving; the British baby is being dressed in a new pair of designer trainers.

Figures of Speech

A figure of speech is an expression which should not be taken literally. For example, 'It's raining cats and dogs' means it is raining heavily, not that animals are falling from the sky!

Make sure you know what the following terms mean, and that you are able to identify uses of them in non-fiction and media texts. Remember that you need to explain how these language features affect the reader's response to the text and its subject matter.

- **Similes:** writers use similes to enable the reader to gain a vivid image of what is being described. A simile compares one thing to another using the words 'like' or 'as', for example…
  - Karen's hair shone like gold.
  - The bag was as light as a feather.
- **Metaphors:** they are used to create the same effect as similes – to build up a vivid image.

A metaphor describes one thing as if it were another. Metaphors never use 'like' or 'as', for example…
- The fog was a grey veil over the city.

- **Imagery:** writers use imagery to paint a picture in the reader's mind and to help them relate to what is being described.
- **Description:** this is most commonly created through the use of adjectives and adverbs. Description often contains imagery that can be very engaging, for example…
  - The crystal clear waves lapped gently at the sheet of smooth, golden sand.

Examiner's Tip

Look out for writers using extended imagery – an image that runs throughout the text.

Techniques in Non-fiction and Media Texts

Structural Techniques

It is important to note the structure of a piece of writing. Structure refers to the way the text is organised, and the way the story or information is developed through the paragraphs. You should note the order of the information in a text. For example, newspaper articles often deliver stories in non-chronological orders: the beginning of the article is the headline and this usually states the outcome of the story (e.g. Man Injured In Knife Attack). The article then explains what happened in the first place to lead to this outcome.

Anecdotes: writers use anecdotes (short, personal stories which are often amusing) to add interest and engage the reader's attention. They are often used to introduce a piece of writing.

Similarly, a piece of writing may begin or end with a particular type of sentence in order to grab the readers' attention, for example…

- **Exclamations:** e.g. 'it's unbelievable!'
- **Questions or rhetorical questions:** e.g. 'who would have thought it?'
- **Imperatives (commands):** e.g. 'get fit this year.'

Sentence length can have an effect on the mood or tone created in a piece of writing. Short sentences

and fragments (part of a sentence, lacking a subject, object or verb) can be very dramatic and attention-grabbing, and are therefore used in texts such as articles and adverts. Long sentences are used in travel brochures, travel books and biographies, as they are effective in descriptive writing.

Presentation Techniques

Presentation can make a big difference to the effect the text has on the reader. Presentation is important because it can assist the purpose of the text.

- **Images and illustrations:** photos, pictures, cartoons, etc. are used primarily to add interest to a text, but what the image shows has a huge impact on the way the reader interprets the text. (Note the image captions as well). Diagrams, maps, graphs, charts etc. are mostly used to make the meaning of information in a text clear. However, they can look quite daunting.
- **Headlines, titles and subheadings:** these break up the text and draw attention to main points.
- **Logos and slogans:** these are used in adverts and leaflets to catch the reader's eye and make him/her remember the product or company.
- **Colours:** certain types of colours can create particular effects, for example, warm colours (e.g. orange, yellow) can help to create a calm, 'friendly' tone in a piece of writing.
- **Bold and italic** are used to make certain parts of the text stand out. Quotes are often italicised.
- **Underlining** can make points stand out, and adds variation and interest to the overall look of the text.
- **Font type and style:** different font sizes and styles add variety to a text, but can often make it look cluttered and unorganised. Different sizes often appear in articles, adverts and leaflets.
- **Upper/lower case:** certain words may appear in upper case letters (e.g. article headlines) to make them stand out, or to make them seem important, dramatic or sensational.
- **Other features:** a text may contain features such as speech bubbles, arrows and borders, which help to create an informal or formal tone.

Exam Preparation

Find examples of these techniques in the texts you have collected. Think about why they have been used.

Recognising Fact and Opinion

When you read non-fiction and media texts, you will come across both facts and opinions and you must be able to distinguish between the two.

Facts are statements that we can prove; things we know for certain are true. Opinions are personal views. Some people will agree with them whereas others will not.

Look at the following four examples of texts:

> The soldiers have been accused of terrible atrocities. They have tortured and degraded the prisoners who now hold them in nothing but contempt.

It is easy to think of this as a factual statement. However, although the first sentence is fact, the second sentence is full of opinion. We know this because the verb 'accused' in the first sentence suggests that things have not been proven. Unless there is proof, it is not a definite fact.

> Anglesey is the best resort in Britain. It has lovely beaches, superb restaurants and excellent facilities.

This text is opinion. Not everybody will agree that Anglesey is the best resort in Britain, or that its beaches are lovely, its restaurants superb, and its facilities excellent.

> The Isle of Anglesey is situated off the north-west coast of Wales, near the Snowdonia mountain range. It is separated from the mainland by the Menai Strait.

This text is fact because the statements can be checked and proved. It is not just someone's opinion.

> When we test cars we always check the security of doors. Our findings paint a worrying picture for car owners and a disgraceful one for car manufacturers.

The first sentence in this text is fact, as it can be checked and proved. However, the second sentence is opinion. The adjectives 'worrying' and 'disgraceful' convey the writer's own views, rather than facts.

How to Differentiate between Fact and Opinion

Certain words signal opinion. Adjectives often signify opinion rather than fact. Similarly, verbs and adverbs such as: seem, appear, suggest, might, may, should, could, would, supposedly, possibly, believe, apparently and allegedly, imply opinion not fact.

Remember that writers frequently use exaggeration (hyperbole) in order to persuade or to create a reaction in the reader. This often includes the use of superlatives (words such as 'best', 'greatest', 'nicest', 'slowest' etc., and the use of 'most …' or 'least…' as in 'most fantastic', 'least expensive'). Superlatives often suggest someone's opinion. For example: 'you are the greatest, most intelligent student in your school'. Is this a fact or an opinion?

Exam Preparation

1. Decide whether each of the following texts shows fact or opinion, and explain your answers.
- Open for business
- The most exciting theme park ride ever!
- Tickets for the Madonna concert sold out within hours of going on sale.
- It should be her best tour to date.

2. Choose a newspaper article from a broadsheet. Highlight six examples of fact and six examples of opinion in the text.

Analysing Language and Structure

Questions in this section of the exam will ask you to write about the way language is employed in a non-fiction or media text. You need to consider:

1. The vocabulary, the language techniques and the structural techniques used.
2. The effect they are intended to have on the reader.
3. How successful you think the writer has been in achieving the intended effect.

This checklist gives you an idea of what to look for when answering questions about how language and structure are used in non-fiction and media texts.

- Purpose: to argue, persuade, advise, inform, explain, describe, analyse, question, entertain or amuse.
- Tone: serious, light-hearted, formal, informal etc.
- Intended audience: teenagers, adults, students, football fans, athletes etc.
- Narrative point of view: biased, impartial, personal, controversial, dramatic or emotional.
- The vocabulary and language techniques that are employed by the writer.
- The sentence types and structures that are employed by the writer.
- The use of fact and opinion.
- The use of persuasive / descriptive / emotive / sensational language.
- Address: first person ('I', 'me', 'us', 'we'), second person ('you') or third person ('it', 'they', 'he', 'she').
- Tense: past, present or future tense, or a combination (see page 78).
- Structure of the text: chronological, non-chronological etc.

Exam Practice

Choose an article in a broadsheet newspaper. Describe how the writer uses language to shape the reader's response.

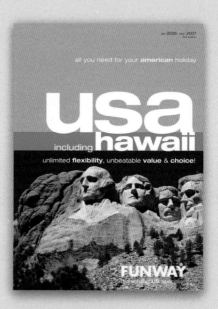

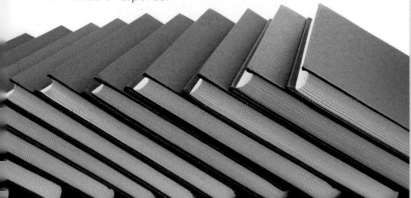

Approaching Texts in the Exam

An Autobiography (Non-fiction Text)

> I stood very still. I couldn't believe what I was seeing. How could he leave me? My heart was ripped out in that split second and all I felt was shock. Pure shock. I had known that the relationship would be difficult and not without problems but to be abandoned without a second thought was almost more than I could bear.

This text includes…

Short sentences, e.g. 'I stood very still', which build up suspense or tension.

Fragments (stress points), e.g. 'Pure shock', which create tension.

Rhetorical questions: 'How could he leave me?' Used to engage and persuade the reader.

Metaphors: '…heart was ripped out…'. Used to make a scene vivid and to create mood and emotion.

Repetition: 'shock. Pure shock'. Used to stress the emotion.

Negative diction: 'shock', 'problems', 'abandoned'. Used to create a serious tone.

To gain an A / A* for your response, you should cover these points in a style similar to the following.

> The collection of short sentences employed by the writer is used effectively to build up tension and suspense. As the writer 'stood very still', the reader is also brought to a halt, wondering what will occur next. The negativity of the next two sentences culminates in the rhetorical question:
>
> 'How could he leave me?'
>
> The character's anger and confusion is portrayed here and the reader is left wondering what has happened. The graphic metaphor and repetition which follow create a vivid image and further emphasise the character's emotions.

A Persuasive Text (Media Text)

> An exceptional value holiday to Austria's Lake District, featuring spectacular scenery and superb sightseeing. With a lovely lakeside location and a host of included excursions, this really is a wonderful combination.

This text includes…

Positive diction, e.g. 'exceptional', 'holiday', 'lovely', 'wonderful', which is used to create a positive tone.

Opinion, rather than fact, to persuade the readers.

Adjectives: 'spectacular' 'superb', 'lovely', 'wonderful'. Used to convince the reader that the scenery is breathtaking.

Adjectival phrases, e.g. 'an exceptional value holiday' and 'wonderful combination', suggest that the holiday is varied and well worth the money.

Alliteration: 'lovely lakeside location'. Used to emphasise certain points, in this case, the attractive lakeside accommodation, and to highlight all the positive aspects of the destination.

To gain an A / A* for your response, you should cover these points in a style similar to the following.

> The holiday brochure text is persuasive and employs the techniques associated with persuasive writing. It is made up of positive diction which creates a positive overall tone.
>
> Opinion is used throughout the text to sound like fact, for example, 'this is an exceptional value holiday'. Actually, fact only appears once in 'a host of included excursions'.
>
> The text is very descriptive, using complex sentences containing adjectives such as 'spectacular', 'superb' and 'lovely' to highlight the beauty of the location, and adjectival phrases such as 'an exceptional value holiday' to reinforce the excellent value of the holiday.
>
> The writer's use of alliteration further emphasises the positive aspects of the Austrian holiday.

Analysing Presentation

Depending on the form of a piece of writing, a range of presentational devices can be used to create impact and assist purpose. In questions about form and presentation you need to comment upon:

1. The presentational devices that are used and the effect they are intended to have on the reader.
2. How successful you think the presentational devices are in achieving the intended effect.

You need to show that you can understand media concepts and comment perceptively on their effect on the reader.

This checklist gives you an idea of what to look for when answering questions about non-fiction and media texts and how they are presented.

- Form: article, leaflet, advert etc.
- Images: analyse their position on the page and their appeal.
- Headlines, titles and subheadings: why have they been used? Are they shocking or dramatic?
- Logos and slogans: what is their appeal? Are they humorous? Do they have any connotations?
- Bold, italics and underlining: think about why they have been used in certain places.
- Font type and size: does the font change throughout the text? What effect does this have?
- Upper / lower case: analyse the effects of using upper case letters, lower case letters, or both.
- Colour: does the text employ a particular colour scheme? Think about whether the colours add to the tone and mood of the text.
- Overall layout: is the presentation eye-catching? Is it clean or cluttered? Does it assist or hinder the purpose of the text?

Approaching Texts in the Exam

The media text (advert) on this page includes...

- **Images:** photos are used to back up the information given in the quotes and to show the facilities. The main image shows friendly students enjoying themselves.
- **Logo / emblem:** this represents the college, and ensures that the reader will remember the college.
- **Colour:** warm colours are used to create a warm, welcoming effect.

To gain an A / A* for your response, you should cover these points in a style similar to the following.

The presentation of the advert assists in its purpose to persuade potential students to enrol at the college, by producing an overall feeling of happiness, enjoyment and a warm welcome. This is created through the use of warm colours (orange and red), and the appealing photos.

The audience is drawn immediately to the main image which shows a group of friendly students having fun at the college. The additional two photos back up the information provided in the students' quotes — computer facilities and approachable tutors.

The college logo ensures that the reader will remember the college at first glance in further publications.

Exam Practice

Choose a magazine article that takes up at least a full page. Describe how the text is presented, why you think it is presented in this way and whether you think the presentation is successful.

Developing Your Answer

An autobiography or biography is an example of a non-fiction text. Study this extract taken from Chapter 1 of William M. Thayer's biography *Abraham Lincoln*. Abraham Lincoln was President of the USA from 1861 to 1865.

> The miserable log cabin in which Abraham Lincoln was born was a floorless, doorless, windowless shanty, situated in one of the most barren and desolate spots of Hardin County, Kentucky. His father made it his home simply because he was too poor to own a better one. Nor was his an exceptional case of penury and want. For the people of that section were generally poor and unlettered, barely able to scrape enough together to keep the wolf of hunger from their abodes.
>
> Here Abraham Lincoln was born February 12th, 1809. His father's name was Thomas Lincoln; his mother's maiden name was Nancy Hanks... They had been married three years when Abraham was born. Their cabin was in that part of Hardin County which is now embraced in La Rue County, a few miles from Hodgensville—on the south fork of Nolin Creek. A perennial spring of water, gushing in silvery brightness from beneath a rock near by, relieved the barrenness of the location, and won for it the somewhat ambitious name—"Rock Spring Farm."

Here is an example of the sort of question you could be asked on a non-fiction text like the one above.

Q. How does Thayer use language to convey an image of the place where Abraham Lincoln was born?

You would be expected to comment upon the following points in your answer.

- Negative phrases in the first paragraph suggest a difficult life in poor conditions, e.g. 'floorless …shanty'. These negative phrases emphasise Lincoln's humble start in life.
- Negative diction, e.g. 'penury', 'want', 'unlettered', suggests how poor and uneducated the people were.
- Adjectives in the first paragraph help to create an image in the reader's mind of the poor living conditions that Lincoln was born into, e.g. 'miserable', 'barren', 'desolate'.

- Rule of three in 'floorless, doorless, windowless shanty' highlights the bad points of Lincoln's childhood home.
- Rhyme of 'floorless, doorless' emphasises the negative adjectives.
- Metaphors, e.g. 'wolf of hunger'. This provides a vivid image of the fear of starvation.
- Diction and phrases in the second paragraph are more positive than in the first, e.g. 'which is now embraced in…', 'brightness'. These positive words and phrases depict a happy life, despite the problems of where the family lived.
- Onomatopoeia, e.g. 'gushing', highlights the fact that the water is the best thing about the location.
- The metaphor towards the end is also positive: 'gushing in silvery brightness'. This suggests some beauty despite the 'barrenness of the location'.
- A sarcastic tone is created in the final sentence with the use of 'the somewhat ambitious name…', which implies that, even though Lincoln's home is described more positively in this paragraph, nothing has really improved.
- Complex sentences are used in order to provide detailed description throughout.

Exam Practice

Combine these points and observations into an exam-standard answer.

Developing Your Answer

Flash Floods Devastate Local Villages

Homes, businesses and lives ruined as flood water rises

Flash floods devastated communities in Derbyshire overnight on Friday. The full extent of the destruction is not yet known, but repairing the damaged property and getting people's lives back to normal could take months, if not years.

Destruction

The floods came after days of persistent rain and gale force winds, not encountered in this part of the country for years.

The situation could not be worse for many residents, whose lives have been washed away in the disruption of the last few days. Charlie Turner, 54, from Leafdale, became one of many victims of the floods following Friday's torrential downpour. He awoke on Saturday to find his home swamped under a metre of water. Further distressing news was awaiting him in nearby Greenham when he went to open the family business, Charlie's Chippie: flood water reached halfway up the walls. Says Charlie, 'My grandfather Charlie opened this chippie in 1960 and we've opened six days a week ever since. I feel like I'm letting down the family name by having to close up'.

Charlie's life has been devastated by the flood and it is likely to take many months for the damage to be repaired.

Widespread Damage

Virtually every resident in Leafdale has a similar story to tell and, although the weather is due to ease this week, this is no consolation to the many whose homes and businesses have already been destroyed.

Single mum-of-two Anna Grayson said, 'I just don't know where to start. We're going to have to stay at my mum's until the repair work can be done on the house. It's just a dreadful situation'.

Many media texts try to persuade the audience or try to gain their sympathy using various persuasive techniques. Study the newspaper article above.

Here is an example of the sort of question you could be asked on a media text such as the one above.

Q. How is language used in this article to gain sympathy for the villagers?

You would be expected to comment upon the following points in your answer.

- The headline uses alliteration in 'flash floods' to highlight the main point of the article. The use of the word 'flash' also implies that it happened so quickly the villagers were unprepared.
- Use of the present tense in the headline and strapline makes the story more immediate / real.
- Rule of three in the strapline emphasises the extent of the devastation caused by the flood.
- Sensational words are used throughout the article for effect, e.g. 'destruction', 'terrible', 'devastated'.
- Repetition of 'devastate', 'devastated' stresses the extent of the problems caused.
- Exaggeration / hyperbole – 'could not be worse...' highlights the futility of the situation.
- The metaphor 'lives washed away' creates an upsetting image in the reader's mind.
- Emotive words are used in the article, e.g. 'victim'.
- The fact that the article uses quotes from people who have been affected by the flood makes it seem more real, and allows the reader to identify with the situation the people face.
- The article focuses in particular on one 'victim of the floods' whose home and business has been damaged. This highlights the extent of the flood damage. A quote from this man is used, which talks about how long his business has been going and how it was founded by his grandfather. This gains sympathy by stressing the family connection.
- Use of 'single mum-of-two' lets readers identify and sympathise with the woman's situation.
- Opinion is used by the writer to sound like fact, e.g. 'it could take months to repair the damage'. This again highlights the extent of the damage and suggests that the people will suffer for a long time.
- Negative diction, e.g. 'damaged', 'worse', 'swamped', 'dreadful', prevails throughout.
- All these features together create a mood of sorrow and downheartedness to make the readers sympathise with the villagers.

Examiner's Tip

Most able students will be able to identify these points so it is how you write the 'E' part of the PEE technique that could mean the difference between a B and an A / A*. In your explanation, write in detail but stay relevant, concise and perceptive.

A diary is a piece of literary non-fiction writing.

Study this extract taken from *Pepys Diary* by Samuel Pepys. It is the diary entry dated September 2 1666 – The Great Fire of London.

> Some of our maids sitting up late last night to get things ready against our feast today, Jane called up about three in the morning, to tell us of a great fire they saw in the City. So I rose, and slipped on my night-gown and went to her window, and thought it to be on the back side of Mark Lane at the farthest; but, being unused to such fires as followed, I thought it far enough off, and so went to bed again, and to sleep. . . . By and by Jane comes and tells me that she hears that above 300 houses have been burned down tonight by the fire we saw, and that it is now burning down all Fish Street, by London Bridge. So I made myself ready presently, and walked to the Tower; and there got up upon one of the high places, ... and there I did see the houses at the end of the bridge all on fire, and an infinite great fire on this and the other side... of the bridge...
>
> So down [I went], with my heart full of trouble, to the Lieutenant of the Tower, who tells me that it began this morning in the King's baker's house in Pudding Lane, and that it hath burned St. Magnus's Church and most part of Fish Street already. So I rode down to the waterside, ... and there saw a lamentable fire ... Everybody endeavouring to remove their goods, and flinging into the river or bringing them into lighters that lay off; poor people staying in their houses as long as till the very fire touched them, and then running into boats, or clambering from one pair of stairs by the waterside to another. And among other things, the poor pigeons, I perceive, were loth to leave their houses, but hovered about the windows and balconies, till they some of them burned their wings and fell down.

Here is an example of the sort of question you could be asked on a non-fiction text like the one above.

Q. How does the writer use language to shape the readers' response?

The following is part of an A / A* standard answer to this question. It demonstrates the type of response that is expected from an A / A* candidate.

The diary is a first person account of what happened and, therefore, we see events through the character's eyes. This enables the reader to share the writer's thoughts and feelings about what is described, and to empathise with him.

From the opening of the text it is apparent that the writer is a man of money, as it is his maids who first tell him of the fires. However, he does feel for the plight of the people affected by the fire, as we see later on in the entry and, as a consequence, the reader shares this plight.

It is written in the present tense, as expected of the diary form, and here it adds to the realism and immediacy of

the text. The reader can share the writer's experiences as he encounters them. He reveals that he is perturbed by the fire, through the metaphor he uses to describe his feelings as he goes to investigate the damage, 'with my heart full of trouble'. This reveals that he is emotionally affected by the fire and its effects.

He describes the 'poor people', trying to save their belongings, and the 'poor pigeons' getting their wings burned. The repetition of the adjective 'poor' is interesting in that it is applied to both the people and the birds. The writer may have used this to show how the fire has affected all: from the inhabitants to the creatures…

Note that in this partial answer, PEE has been used appropriately, the correct technical terms have been applied, there is a reference to the form of the writing (i.e. a diary), and the writer has made personal, perceptive observations, for example, the word 'poor' and the comments with it.

Developing Your Answer

We have already seen the kind of language and stylistic features you need to comment upon in order to achieve a top grade. For a question about presentation, you must refer in detail to all aspects of presentation and, if appropriate, aspects of structure.

Study the page below, taken from the *Funway* holiday brochure: *USA including Hawaii.*

Here is an example of the sort of question about presentation that you could be asked on a media text like the one below.

Q. In what way does the presentation of this travel brochure page help to persuade its readers to visit America's West?

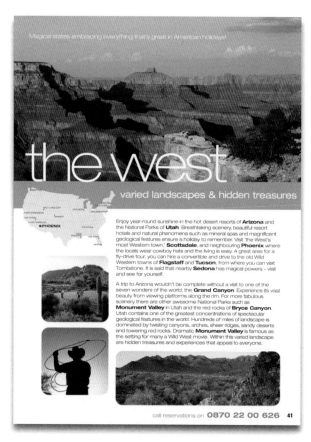

The following is part of an A/A* standard answer to the question opposite. It demonstrates the type of response expected from an A/A* candidate.

The presentation of the information given on this travel brochure page reinforces its persuasive tone. The text appears beautifully on the page, evoking the images traditionally associated with the Grand Canyon and the American Wild West of cowboy films, which makes readers think a holiday there will indeed be everything they ever thought it could be.

The title refers to the 'magical states,' and the images throughout the text reinforce this portrayal. This exclamatory sentence stresses the main title and prepares us to be amazed.

The reader's eye is immediately drawn to the spectacular shot of the Grand Canyon. The richness of the colours gives it an almost dream-like quality, just as the abundance of positive adjectives in the passage depicts the place as 'magical' as it is so beautiful. The shadows in the main image represent the 'hidden treasures' in the strapline, and the colours convey warmth and sunshine.

The idea of the Wild West runs throughout the

passage: there are two references to it in the text and an image portraying the stereotypical view of a cowboy, complete with Stetson and lasso.

The beauty that is depicted in the text is further reinforced by the images around it. Similarly, as the text ascertains that the West appeals to everyone, so too do the images: from the men playing golf, to the panoramic landscape shots that would appeal to many people, whatever their particular interests. The variety of the images also attests to the statement in the strapline 'varied landscapes'.

A map is also used on the page to provide a quick reference for readers of where the area is. Its colour is fitting with the other colours on the page to symbolise the heat and sunshine.

Within the main text, a number of words are depicted in bold; the words in bold are all the places that can be visited. Putting the words in bold not only makes them stand out, but also shows, at a glance, the number of places available to visit through this travel company.

Exam Practice and Exam Tips

Read the two media texts on this page.

1. Comment on the language devices used in the 'Fat Combat' advert to persuade readers to join.
2. How does the writer use language in the 'Weight Loss' article to shape the reader's response?
3. Compare how language is used in both the texts.
4. How effective is the presentation of the advert and the article?

Exam Tips

In order to perform at your best in the exam, you need to be in control of your whole approach to it and know the kind of questions you could get.

Before the exam, make sure that you…

- learn the key terms covered in this section of the guide
- work through all the exam preparation and exam practice tasks in this section of the guide
- practise writing to the time limits of the exam; try to work through as many past papers as possible
- read a variety of non-fiction and media texts and highlight interesting stylistic devices.

In the exam, make sure that you…

- read the questions carefully and work out how long to spend on each question according to the marks available
- plan your answers before you start writing
- answer the question asked
- use the PEE technique
- refer to language, structure and presentation.

Weight Loss
The Fact and the Fantasy

We all want to lose a little weight this New Year, and we may all think that we know how. Many given 'facts' about weight loss, however, are complete horse feathers…

Fantasy
Diets really work for permanent weight loss.

Fact
Most diets are codswallop; those that do work should really only be used to kickstart a healthy, long-term eating plan. Any diet that seriously restricts your calorie intake or limits the number of foods you can eat is extremely difficult to stick to; if you then go back to eating normally you will simply regain the weight. Avoid diets like the Atkins plan; diets like this do not give you all the nutrients your body needs and will only result in health problems. Much better is to get into a balanced, healthy eating habit.

Fantasy
If I want to lose weight I must cut my favourite sweet or fatty foods out of my diet.

Fact
That's not strictly true. In order to lose weight you must be burning more calories than you are eating; while sweet or fatty foods are generally higher in calories than healthier options, provided your calories intake remains lower than your body's minimum energy requirement you can eat whatever you like. After all, a pattern of eating with absolutely no treats at all would be a very grim existence – and who wants to be thin and miserable?

Fantasy
Skipping meals will help me to lose weight.

Fact
Again, complete bunkum. Obviously, not eating at all will lower your calorie intake, but this is the silliest way to do it. Furthermore studies show that people who eat smaller portions more often find it easier to lose weight, because they are much better at managing their appetites.

Fantasy
Eating after 8pm will make me put on weight.

Fact
Weight loss / gain depends on the balance between your daily intake of calories and your daily energy requirement (of course, this requirement is higher the more physical activity you do, so figure your exercise into the equation). What time of day you eat has no effect at all – your body will store surplus calories as fat either way.

Fantasy
Natural or herbal weight-loss products are safe and effective.

Fact
There is no easy way to lose weight, unfortunately. Weight-loss products can help, but even products claiming to be 'natural' can be dangerous, since they are rarely rigorously tested and can have serious side effects on your body. Lose weight in the way that is 100% natural: eat fresh, healthy food and push it through your body with some exhilarating exercise – you'll soon see and feel the difference. Fact!

Writing to Argue, Persuade or Advise

The Exam Question

In Section B of Paper 1 you will be tested on your ability to write for a particular purpose. You will have a choice of three or four questions. Each one will ask you to produce a different kind of writing. You will have 45 minutes to complete **one** question of your choice. You should spend 10 minutes of this time planning and checking your answer. The questions will cover three different types of writing:

- writing to argue
- writing to persuade
- writing to advise.

The choice of questions usually includes one for each type of writing and a further question which combines two of the three types (e.g. argue and persuade).

What is the examiner looking for?

Each question on the exam paper will require a different style of writing for which you will need to know the conventions or rules. In addition, regardless of which question you choose to answer, the examiner will always be looking for generic skills that are common to writing.

The specific skills for producing the different styles of writing are covered later in this chapter. The generic writing skills required to gain a grade A or A* are listed here. Many are the same as for Section B of

Paper 2 (writing to inform, explain or describe – see page 72). You must be able to demonstrate that you can do the following.

- Write clearly for the specified purpose and audience.
- Communicate and express your ideas clearly and imaginatively in writing.
- Confidently use a variety of effective sentence structures, extensive vocabulary and means of expression.
- Use a wide range of grammatical constructions accurately.
- Demonstrate accurate punctuation and correct spelling (see pages 4–5).
- Construct paragraphs well and link them to clarify the organisation of the writing as a whole.
- Develop and display a strong personal style.
- Produce writing that has clear structure and organisation.
- Produce writing that is consistently coherent and logical.
- Write effectively in different forms (letters, leaflets etc.), adapting them to suit different audiences and purposes.
- Ensure that content and style are appropriate to the purpose, audience and form.
- Use Standard English confidently.
- Present your answer clearly in neat handwriting so that the examiner can easily read and understand it.

Writing to Argue

96 Oak Close
Southampton

Daily News
Main Street
Southampton

Dear Editor

I am writing to voice my strong opposition to your article about prohibiting ball games in the park. I believe this campaign is absolutely deplorable.

With levels of obesity amongst children on the increase, surely we should be encouraging exercise?

Some people might argue that ball games can be dangerous, but children have always played in the park and I believe it essential that they continue to do so.

Yours faithfully

D Jeffries

Mrs D Jeffries

Writing to Persuade

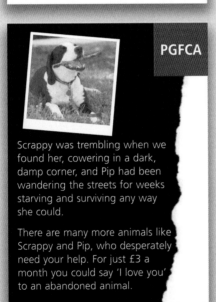

PGFCA

Scrappy was trembling when we found her, cowering in a dark, damp corner, and Pip had been wandering the streets for weeks starving and surviving any way she could.

There are many more animals like Scrappy and Pip, who desperately need your help. For just £3 a month you could say 'I love you' to an abandoned animal.

Writing to Advise

Success in...

Job Interviews

Remember that first impressions can count for a lot, so make sure you dress  smartly and appropriately for the workplace. Be friendly, smile confidently and shake hands with assurance.

Try to have at least one or two questions ready to ask your interviewer at the end of the interview, however, it is not recommended that you enquire about the salary at this stage.

Writing to Argue

Arguing involves expressing a point of view as clearly and effectively as possible. This will usually include presenting evidence and a series of reasons for your argument. You must…

- express a point of view clearly
- be aware that someone else has a different point of view
- try to achieve a balanced argument. Don't just put forward your own view.

The letter opposite, written to a newspaper, is a short, simple example of writing to argue.

Writing to Persuade

Persuading involves making your readers agree with a particular point of view, or making them feel a certain way. This might involve argument, but it will usually also involve other methods of trying to influence people's feelings. You must…

- try to encourage someone to do something they might not want to do
- understand why they might not want to do it
- use different techniques to try to persuade them.

The charity advert opposite is a short, simple example of writing to persuade.

Writing to Advise

Advising involves giving someone help by telling them clearly how to do something in the easiest, quickest or best way. You must…

- write in a personal, encouraging way
- write clearly and logically in a way that is easy to understand
- write in role as a person who knows the answers.

The extract opposite, from a leaflet about how to be successful in job interviews, is a short, simple example of writing to advise.

There may be elements of other types of writing in your chosen question as well as the one specified; for example, in order to write a letter persuading somebody to agree with you on an issue, you may need to include your argument for the issue. However, always make sure you focus on the type of writing that appears in bold print in the question; this is the type of writing you are being asked to demonstrate.

Purpose, Audience, Form and Language

The first things you need to know before you start to write are…

- **what is the purpose of the writing?**
- **who is your audience?**

Purpose

We know that the purpose of the writing in this section of the exam is to argue, persuade or advise (or a combination of them). You may be asked to…

- argue for or against something
- persuade someone to do or not to do something
- advise someone on the best, easiest, quickest or most effective way to do something.

Here are some examples of the type of questions you could be asked on arguing, persuading or advising.

Q. Write a letter to your local Member of Parliament, in which you **argue** against the lack of facilities for young people in your area, and **persuade** him / her that more facilities should be made available.

Q. Write an article for the school magazine in which you **advise** students on the importance of being healthy and how to maintain a healthy lifestyle.

The purpose of each question is obvious as the key words are printed in bold. You have no excuse for misunderstanding the question.

The first question opposite could be answered with information based on actual facts about the facilities where you live, or made-up information. You would write from your own perspective, but you could include experiences of your friends and the facilities where they live, as well as your own experiences with the facilities in different areas you have visited. You could suggest solutions. Remember that the focus is on arguing and persuading so you need to clearly express your view, try to achieve a balanced argument and try to make the audience agree with you.

The second question asks you to provide facts and information in a way that will help the audience. You would write from a personal viewpoint, in role as an expert. You could focus on advising about healthy eating, exercise, the dangers of smoking, drinking and drugs, or a combination of them. Beware of simply giving information; the emphasis is on advising, not informing, so you need to write clearly in an encouraging (but not patronising) tone.

Audience

There are many possible audiences that you may be asked to write to / for. Here are some examples (there are many more):

- teenagers
- adults
- students at your school
- the local council
- teachers
- MPs.

When you are writing for a specific audience, consider the audience's age, gender, social class, interests, background, culture and your relationship with them. All these factors will affect the language and style that you employ in your writing.

Form

Every piece of writing has a particular form. The form refers to how the writing is presented. In this section of the exam you are usually asked to write in a specific form, for example...

- a holiday brochure extract
- a newspaper report
- a magazine article
- a formal or informal letter
- a leaflet
- an advice sheet
- a news sheet
- an on-line page or email.

(See pages 37–39.)

Language and Style

The language you use in your writing must be appropriate for the audience you are aiming at so you need to make sure you adopt the right register (tone). Register is the tone of voice and the level of formality you use when speaking and writing. You wouldn't speak to your teachers in the same way you speak to your brothers and sisters, so the register needs to be chosen carefully.

The audience is the major factor that influences your choice of register, however, the purpose and form will also affect the type of language you use. Whatever the purpose of your writing, you should adopt the language devices and techniques appropriate to that purpose (see pages 40, 42 and 44).

You must consider your use of vocabulary, grammar and punctuation, and various language techniques in order to make your style of writing appropriate to the audience, purpose and form. For example...

Style: should your style be formal or informal? Personal or impersonal? Factual or emotive?

Grammar and punctuation: should you use direct personal address (use of the second person personal pronoun 'you')? Contractions (e.g. don't, you'll)? Active or passive voice? Imperatives, questions or exclamations? Modal verbs? Simple, compound or complex sentences?

Language techniques: should you include language devices such as puns, alliteration or rule of three?

(For more on language and register, see page 75.)

Here is a good mnemonic which might help you to remember the main points to consider when answering the exam question:
F – Form
L – Language, style and register
A – Audience
P – Purpose

When you have chosen which exam question you are going to answer, underline the key words in order to fill in the FLAP mnemonic, for example...

Q. Write a letter to your head teacher **persuading** him / her to give you an extra week to complete your coursework.

Form   – letter
Language – formal
Audience – your head teacher
Purpose – persuade

Exam Preparation

Underline the key words in the following questions and then use the FLAP technique to identify the form, language, audience and purpose.

Q. Write a speech to be made at a governors' meeting where you, as a student, try to **persuade** the governors to abolish school uniform.

Q. Write the text for a leaflet **persuading** local residents to vote against the destruction of woodland for the building of 100 new houses.

Planning Your Answer

In the exam you should spend about five minutes planning and sequencing ideas for your answer. You will not get extra marks for planning but examiners believe that it helps students to write organised and well-structured pieces which will, in turn, help them to get higher grades. At grade A and above, examiners will expect your writing to be logical and crafted.

Planning is a good way to logically structure your answer before you start writing.

Planning Techniques

Some students like to brainstorm their ideas; others like to make lists. It doesn't matter which technique you use to plan, as long as you plan effectively. Planning just for the sake of it is a waste of time.

Read the following question, then look at the plan that follows.

Q. Imagine you are a sports personality. Write an **advice** sheet for young people about what it takes to become successful.

Firstly, think about the main ideas for your answer:
- determination
- hard work
- practice
- positive thinking.

You may then want to fill out these ideas, for example...
- determination:
  - sacrifices – missing parties, getting early nights, spending weekends practising
  - setting goals and targets
  - believing in yourself.

As you plan through each section you may realise that some of your ideas are in the wrong section. For example, 'believing in yourself' is partly to do with being determined but it is more likely to go in the 'positive thinking' section. This is why planning is so beneficial: it prevents you from getting your ideas mixed up and repeating yourself.

Planning also helps to combat nerves by putting you in control of the question and taking a few minutes to think positively about your answer before writing.

Some students don't think they have time in the exam to plan effectively, however, this is not true: it is possible to create a very useful plan in about three minutes.

Exam Preparation

Plan effective answers to the following questions in five minutes. You may not even need that much time.

Q. Imagine that you are a sports personality. Write an **advice** sheet for young people about what it takes to become successful.

Q. Write a letter to the school governors to try to **persuade** them to abolish school uniform.

Structure: Sentences

In order to achieve a top grade in the writing exam, you need to demonstrate that you can use different grammatical structures. There are a number of different sentence structures and types of sentence; you should try to use all of them in your writing.

Simple Sentences

A simple sentence contains one main clause. A main clause usually consists of a subject (which is a noun), a verb and an object (which is a noun), for example…
- the cat (subject) sat (verb) on the mat (object).

Simple sentences give information quickly and clearly. They are good for grabbing the audience's attention and are often used in persuasive adverts. Look at the first two sentences in this advert.
- You need a new car. You are intimidated by car salesmen. Come to cars4women where there are sympathetic saleswomen who understand how difficult it can be choosing the right car.

Compound Sentences

A compound sentence consists of two or more simple sentences linked with a conjunction, such as 'and', 'but' etc. Each clause in a compound sentence makes sense on its own and each is of equal importance, for example…
- I went to the shop and I bought some milk.
- We went to the beach but it rained.
- Reece played the guitar well so he joined a band.

Complex Sentences

A complex sentence consists of a main clause and one or more other clauses which are of lesser importance than the main clause. These lesser clauses are called **subordinate clauses**. Subordinate clauses cannot make sense on their own, but the rest of the sentence can make sense without them. Subordinate clauses occur most frequently in long sentences and are often introduced with connectives such as 'that', 'because', 'when', 'after', 'although', 'as', 'rather than', 'in order to' and 'so that', for example…
- After my children started school, I found that I had lots of free time.
- Although we argue, I get on really well with my parents.

The more complex a piece of writing is the more subordinate clauses it will have in its sentences.

A subordinate clause can come at the beginning of a sentence; it is known as a **fronted clause**, for example…
- Despite knowing I was wrong, I still continued with the argument.
- Although we are behind schedule, we should not go over budget.

A subordinate clause can be embedded within a sentence; it is called an **embedded clause**, for example…
- Charlie, when he wasn't climbing up the curtains, was a good cat.
- This new car, which is more expensive than the old model, has air conditioning.

Sentence Types

1. **Statements** are used most often. They are used in all types of writing, for example…
   - The boy went to town.

2. **Questions (normal and rhetorical)** usually address the reader directly and are often used in argumentative and persuasive writing to highlight an issue, for example…
   - What can you do about this?

3. **Imperatives (commands)** give instruction, advice or warning and tend to begin with a verb. They are often used in writing to advise, for example…
   - Feed your dog twice a day.
   - Go and talk to someone you can trust.

4. **Exclamations** are used for emphasis. An exclamation is shown by the exclamation mark at the end of the sentence. They are often used in argumentative and persuasive writing, for example…
   - It's so unfair!

5. **Conditional sentences** are used to express action depending on certain conditions. They are often used in writing to persuade or advise, for example…
   - If you let me go out, I'll clean the bathroom.
   - If that doesn't work, try talking to your teacher.

Examiner's Tip

Try to use simple, compound and complex sentences in your writing, as well as suitable sentence types (statements, imperatives etc.). You should also vary the lengths of your sentences; this can be very effective.

Structure: Paragraphs

The examiner will be looking for evidence of paragraphs when marking your writing paper. Paragraphs are used to organise pieces of writing: they are sets of sentences which have related ideas or subjects. Make sure you use them in every piece of writing you do. You can show paragraphs in your writing either by leaving a line before starting a new paragraph, or by indenting the text when you start a new paragraph.

Using paragraphs means you don't end up with a solid block of text, and it allows you to present your writing in an organised way so that your ideas are easier to follow. You should start a new paragraph every time you have a change of time, speaker, place, idea or person.

Beginning and Ending

Every piece of writing will have an opening paragraph and a concluding paragraph. The opening paragraph should make your intentions clear to the audience, and the concluding paragraph should summarise the main points of your writing.

A good opening paragraph in writing to persuade might flatter or compliment the reader to gain their interest. A good opening paragraph in writing to advise might offer a compliment or a sympathetic phrase to the reader to gain their trust and confidence.

Look at the example opposite of a good opening paragraph for writing to persuade. The writer gains the audience's attention and trust by complimenting his/her home and empathising with him/her. The writer then hints at the purpose of the writing with a rhetorical question to introduce what follows.

A good opening paragraph in writing to argue will describe your intentions and views whilst recognising others.

Look at the example opposite of a good opening paragraph for writing to argue. The writer states her view clearly, and recognises the opposing point.

A good conclusion to any piece of writing will summarise the main points you have made in your writing.

Look at the example opposite of a good concluding paragraph to the letter. The writer opens the final paragraph well with 'In conclusion' and goes on to summarise the main points of the letter, including the opposing viewpoint. She rounds off the letter well by suggesting that she expects a response.

Writing to Persuade

Holmfirth conservatories

Your home is your haven, your favourite place to be – a special place for you, your family and your memories. Why not make it even more special by extending with a beautiful classic conservatory?

Writing to Argue

96 Oak Close,
Southampton.

Daily News,
1 Main Street,
Southampton

Dear Sir / Madam

   I am writing to you to voice my opposition to the building of a supermarket on the recreation ground in the village. Whilst I am strongly against this proposal, I do recognise that there are some equally important issues about the lack of a supermarket in the village that need addressing.

A Conclusion

   In conclusion, I feel I have shown that the recreation ground is vital to the village in many ways and, whilst the problems of the elderly and access to supermarkets do need addressing, I feel that this cannot be at the expense of village life. I hope you take my proposals on board and I look forward to hearing from you shortly.

Yours faithfully

D Jeffries

Mrs D Jeffries

Language

Connectives

Connectives (or discourse markers) are words and phrases that link paragraphs, sentences, or clauses within sentences (e.g. although, because). The examiners will expect you to use connectives to link your writing and make it fluent. You can use connectives in the following ways:

1 At the beginning of a sentence, for example…
- **Although** it can be dangerous, skiing is great fun.

2 In the middle of a sentence, for example…
- The programme has been popular with teenagers **despite** the fact that it is on after 11.00pm.

3 To connect paragraphs, for example…
- We left early for the long journey home. **Finally,** back at home in good time, we were able to relax and go to bed.

Connectives in Writing to Argue

Connectives can be particularly useful in writing to argue for or against something. They can be used effectively to open and close an argument, for example…
- **Firstly,** I would like to note that…
- **In conclusion** I feel that…

Connectives in Writing to Persuade or Advise

Connectives can be useful in writing to persuade or advise because they allow you to state the problem and then connect it naturally to the subject you are persuading or advising the audience on,

for example…
- It may prove rather stressful, **whereas** choosing to buy from us…
- This can be a problem. **Consequently,** I felt it might help you to…

Here is a list of connectives. It may help you to learn some of them so that you can use them effectively in the exam. Try to think of some less commonly used connectives to put into your writing.

Clearly	Notably	However
Similarly	Therefore	Secondly
Equally	Even so	Most importantly
As	For example	In any case
Naturally	In addition	In conclusion
In fact	Finally	Despite this
Alternatively	Although	Evidently
Consequently	Thus	Obviously
Due to	Alternatively	Nevertheless
Moreover	Furthermore	Whereas

Exam Preparation

Write a short letter to a newspaper summarising your argument about an issue you feel strongly about (e.g. the environment, crime). Use at least one connective in all of the following places:
- to open a sentence
- to connect a sentence
- to open a paragraph
- in your introduction
- in your conclusion.

Language

Verbs

One of the language features that examiners will be looking for is your use of verbs. Verbs are 'doing' words, e.g. run, laugh, sing. We use verbs in our writing all the time. However, there are special forms of verbs that will help you to gain more marks.

Infinitives

The infinitive of a verb is the 'root' of the verb (i.e. without any endings for tense or person). It usually includes 'to' (e.g. to run, to laugh, to sing). Infinitives can create a formal tone when used in writing and so they are useful in writing to argue, persuade or advise, for example…

- It is important **to object** to these ridiculous proposals.
- We need **to help** these people.
- I think it would help you **to talk** openly to someone.

Examiner's Tip

'Split infinitives' are seen by some as grammatically incorrect. To 'split' the infinitive means to split 'to' and the verb (by adding an adverb), e.g. '**to** quickly **run**', (instead of '**to run** quickly'). Although split infinitives are widely used (e.g. 'to boldly go', made famous by *Star Trek*), some examiners still view them as incorrect, so if you use an infinitive in your writing, try not to split it!

Modal Verbs

Modal verbs are used to help the main verb; another verb is always needed. The modal verbs are: can, will, shall, may, could, would, should, might, must, ought to.

Modals can alter the tone of writing and can be used for a variety of effects:

- to make something sound more polite (often by turning it into a question). Compare 'give the dog his dinner', to 'could you give the dog his dinner?'
- to highlight or give emphasis to what you want to say, e.g. 'it should be easy to operate', 'it will appeal to young people'.

Modals are used when giving advice, for example…
- You should speak to another adult.
- Perhaps you could ask your friends for help.

Active and Passive Voices

Sentences can be active or passive, depending on whether the verb form is active or passive. Whether you use the active or the passive voice in your sentences can make a difference to the tone of the writing. When the subject of the sentence is doing the action, the sentence is active. When the subject of the sentence is having something done to them, the sentence is passive. Look at the following sentences:
- Ben broke the window.   **Active**
- The window was broken by Ben. **Passive**

The passive voice emphasises the object (in this case the window), turning it into the subject, and creates an impersonal and formal tone. Using the passive means that the original subject can be left out, e.g. 'The window was broken'.

In writing to argue, persuade and advise, the active voice tends to be used the most as these types of writing are quite direct and personal.

Form

Articles

It is likely that you will get a question in the exam which asks you to write an article for a newspaper, magazine or Internet site.

Features of Articles

Newspapers and magazines use a variety of techniques to grab the audience's attention; this includes the structure of the article and the language used in it.

- Each article has a **headline** which summarises the content of the article and / or uses a particular feature designed to intrigue, shock, amuse, persuade etc.
- Main or longer articles also have a **strapline** which further explains the content of the article and draws attention to its main points.
- **Sub-headings** are used to separate the text, particularly in long articles, where they may appear as headings to photographs / illustrations.
- **Direct quotes** and **reported speech** from eyewitnesses, victims, experts etc. add more detail and interest to an article. Name, age, occupation and relevance to the story are often given. This is known as non-essential information.

Structure of Articles

Headline: uses present tense, uses language devices.
First paragraph: should be 25 words or less, must include who, what, where and when.
Second paragraph: should relate to the first paragraph but give more detail.
Third and following paragraphs: should give additional information and explanation (why and how).

Who	What	Where	When

Bin Man Wins Wonga Award!

He's not rubbish!

Yesterday bin man Andy Smith, 41, controversially won the prestigious WONGA music award in a star-studded celebrity ceremony in London.

Alliteration in headline	Pun establishes he is good	Establishes controversy	Sibilance in first paragraph

Examiner's Tip

Newspaper and magazine articles are usually written in columns. However, you should not attempt to write your article in columns; stick to paragraphs – these are what the examiner wants to see.

Style

Reports / articles are generally written in the past tense, as they are telling the audience what happened. But note that headlines almost always use the present tense: this is to make the story more immediate.

Newspaper and magazine articles are full of emotive and sensational language. Emotive language is used to try to influence the audience's feelings. Sensational language is dramatic language to make a piece more exciting, more vivid or more engrossing.

The following language techniques are frequently used in articles to grab the audience's attention. You should try to utilise such features in your writing.

Pun / play on words, e.g. 'She's Parking Mad!'
Rhetorical questions, e.g. 'Do you want this man looking after your children?'
Rhyme, e.g. 'Fame Game Shame'
Alliteration, e.g. 'Mum Mugged for Mobile'
Sibilance, e.g. 'School Salmonella Scare'

Form

FATHER FIGHTS SHARK IN HOLIDAY ATTACK HORROR

A father of three fought off a terrifying shark which had targeted his youngest child during a family holiday in Australia last week.

Brave Graham Bennett was swimming in the sea off the coast of Eastern Australia last Sunday when he spotted the menacing beast slicing through the waves towards a group of young children, which included his son Steven, 9.

Local lifeguards have told how courageous Bennett risked his life to save the children.

Holiday Hero

Janet Peterson, whose daughter, Chloe, was playing in the sea at the time, gushed, *'Graham is our hero! I can't bear to think what could have happened if he hadn't been there'.*

- Present tense in headline
- Alliteration of 'f' and 'h' in headline
- Sensational language: 'attack', 'menacing beast'
- Emotive language: 'horror', 'gushed'
- Alliteration in sub-heading: 'Holiday Hero'
- First paragraph: less than 25 words, gives who, what, where, when
- Second paragraph goes into more detail
- Direct quote used

Note how linguistic features are used in the newspaper article above to achieve its purpose.

Exam Preparation

Write a strapline and the first three paragraphs of a newspaper article based on the headline 'Man found alive after missing for two years'. Use appropriate language, style and language devices.

Exam Practice

Complete the following newspaper article. Write with a view to persuading the paper's audience that Andy deserves the award.

> Bin Man Wins Wonga Award!
> He's not rubbish!
> Yesterday bin man Andy Smith, 41, controversially won the prestigious WONGA music award in a star-studded celebrity ceremony in London.

Leaflets

You may be asked to write the text for a leaflet or information sheet. (See page 82 for more on leaflets). This is usually to persuade or advise.

Leaflets usually contain a mixture of facts and opinions. A fact is something that can be proven to be true. An opinion is someone's viewpoint (see page 19).

Techniques for Writing Leaflets

- Create an effective heading / headline (use the language devices listed on page 37), for example, Stop Smoking Today!
- Catch the audience's attention with the first paragraph: use a variety of sentence types and structures.
- Use sub-headings to guide the audience through the text and lead them to the important points.
- Use a mixture of fact and opinion – use adjectives, adverbs and superlatives where appropriate.

Examiner's Tip

The examiner wants to see that you can write well in English, not that you can make your answer paper look like a leaflet. Do not produce illustrations, fold your paper or write in columns. You can use bullet points, but do not use them excessively. Organise your work into structured paragraphs.

Exam Practice

Q. Write the text for a leaflet for an environmental group who want to **advise** homeowners on how to help the environment.

Speech Writing

Speeches are good examples of writing to persuade or argue. For example, a political speech is written to try to persuade the audience to vote for that party. There are many techniques used by speech writers to hold the audience's interest and to try to influence their views.

Speeches must be organised into clear paragraphs and should contain language which grabs the audience's attention. However, speeches are written to be read aloud so you need to use language devices that can be heard.

Language Devices for Speeches

- **Rule of three** is frequently used in speeches. It may be three questions, three rhetorical questions, three points etc. Rule of three is very good at emphasising a point and is very effective when spoken.
- **Repetition** emphasises words and phrases and makes them stick in the audience's minds.
- **Parallelism** involves the repetition of sentences with similar use of vocabulary, e.g. 'I have a dream that one day this nation… I have a dream that one day on the red hills…'
- **Contrasts and opposites** are used for emphasis by putting one word or idea next to a different word or idea, e.g. 'It is important we reward the good students, not just punish the bad'. This contrasts the good with the bad, and reward with punishment.
- **Rhetorical questions** address the audience in a way that makes them feel involved.
- **Use of personal pronouns**, possessive pronouns and friendly terms of address (e.g. 'Friends', 'Fellow workers') break down barriers between the speaker and the audience. The use of the first person pronoun 'I' also indicates the speaker's authority.

- **Emotive and sensational language** can make the audience feel a certain way, e.g. sympathetic, shocked, guilty, excited, enthusiastic etc.
- **Lists** can emphasise how many/few there are of something, e.g. listing countries in the world where millions live in poverty highlights the extent of the problem.
- **Superlatives** are effective as they can stress the best, worst, most or least of something, e.g. 'Last year we had the highest costs but the lowest returns'.
- **Alliteration** can indicate the speaker's feelings: harsh 't' sounds could convey anger or frustration, while soft 'm' sounds might imply sympathy or respect, e.g. 'We will not tolerate tyrants in our trade'.

Exam Practice

Q. Write a speech to be presented to your classmates where you **argue** for the right to vote at 16.

Writing to Argue

Writing an argument means expressing your opinion – what you think and feel about an issue.

In order to achieve a top grade, you need to cover the following three main points:

1. **Argument:** express your opinion about an issue.
2. **Counter argument:** be aware that someone else has a different point of view and try to discredit that viewpoint.
3. **Balance:** try to achieve a balanced argument.

Structuring Your Argument

1. Introduction to clearly state your opinion.
2. Main body of writing to include your argument (giving reasons for it), an acknowledgement of the other argument/opinion, counter argument (say why you believe it is wrong), and evidence.
3. Conclusion to summarise your argument.

Techniques in Writing to Argue

Here are some techniques you could use to make your argument as convincing as possible. Note that many of the techniques used in writing to argue are the same as those used in writing to persuade; these two types of writing are closely linked.

- **Positive opening** to clearly state your opinion.
- **Evidence and justification** to give structure and reasoning to your opinion (use the PEE technique).
- Suitable **connectives** to…
  - give your piece structure, e.g. firstly, secondly
  - to express cause and effect, e.g. consequently
  - to express comparisons to link your arguments, e.g. however, on the other hand.
- **Rhetorical questions** to involve the reader and to highlight the issue by asking a question to which the answer is obvious.
- **Comparative devices** such as similes and metaphors to emphasise your main points, making them stand out by attaching particular connotations.
- **Exaggeration** to catch the reader's attention and to encourage them to agree with you.
- **Rule of three** to stress the reasons for your argument in a way that stands out.
- **Personal tone:** a personal perspective is important in arguing. You may even include personal anecdotes (see page 83) if appropriate.
- A series of **structured paragraphs** which give an organised argument and counter argument.
- **Present tense** to make your argument seem more immediate and, therefore, more pressing.
- **Personal pronouns** to create a personal tone and make your argument seem more believable. Use of personal pronouns can also help to establish a good relationship between the writer and the audience.
- **Exclamations** to stress the importance of your argument, or to discredit the other argument.
- **Infinitive verb forms** to create a formal tone.
- **Colons** can make a point more directly by creating a sharp pause before explaining the point.
- **Semi-colons** are useful for listing the points of your argument. A colon introduces the list and semi-colons break up the items listed.
- A **clear conclusion** to summarise and re-state your opinion.

Look at the following example of writing to argue. It is the text for a speech to be read by a student arguing against smoking in schools.
(In the exam you will be expected to write more than this.)

This speech gives the speaker's opinion clearly in the introduction. Reasons are given to back up the speaker's argument and, whilst the counter argument is acknowledged, it is also discredited, giving more strength to the speaker's argument. The conclusion briefly summarises the argument.

Exam Practice

Q. Write an article for a teenagers' magazine in which you **argue** against people wearing clothes and accessories made out of real animal fur.

First and second person pronouns give a personal tone	Fellow students,

I am speaking to you today to give you my views on smoking. It is an expensive, unattractive and unhealthy habit. Smoking destroys the heart and lungs causing heart attacks and angina; it causes blood clots that can lead to amputations; it makes people look old and causes bad breath. It could even kill. |

Fellow students,

I am speaking to you today to give you my views on smoking. It is an expensive, unattractive and unhealthy habit. Smoking destroys the heart and lungs causing heart attacks and angina; it causes blood clots that can lead to amputations; it makes people look old and causes bad breath. It could even kill.

The law tries to protect young people from smoking by making the legal age for buying cigarettes 16; this is because smoking has a terrible effect on people's lives. I believe that it is school's job to protect young people too.

However, some students believe it is their right to smoke – that they have freedom of choice, especially once they are 16. I am sure you will agree that these arguments are immature. Firstly, most children who smoke in school are not 16 and, even if they were, smoking is illegal in schools, therefore, no-one has the right. Furthermore, we all know the harm that passive smoking can do.

Consequently, we are starting a Shout out! campaign designed to help create a better environment for ourselves at school. There are three things we plan to do: have more teacher patrols in the toilets, have stricter sanctions against people caught smoking, and encourage you to shout out and let us know who is smoking.

Some people may say it goes against the students' code of ethics to inform upon other students, but clearly this is not true. I believe that it is our duty to eradicate smoking: the smokers are breaking the law. What right have they to damage our health and pollute our environment?

Next week there will be an assembly telling you how to join the campaign. Help to stop this destructive plague in our school: join our campaign today!

I believe we must act now to ensure a more pleasant environment for all students. So shout out against smoking! Make your voice heard!

Annotations (left margin):

- First and second person pronouns give a personal tone
- Present tense makes the argument more urgent
- Positive opening statement
- Comparative device – metaphor
- Rule of three
- Infinitive verb forms
- Discrediting the other opinion
- Suitable connectives
- Rhetorical questions involve the audience
- Exclamations
- PEE
- Use of colons and semi-colons

Writing to Persuade

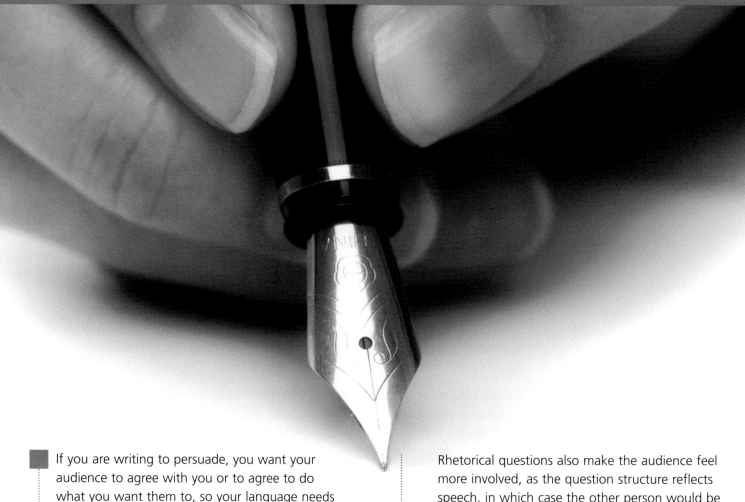

If you are writing to persuade, you want your audience to agree with you or to agree to do what you want them to, so your language needs to represent this. There is a variety of language techniques you can use when writing persuasively.

Techniques in Writing to Persuade

Here is a summary of some of the techniques you could use to make your writing effective as a persuasive piece. Note that many of the techniques used in writing to persuade are the same as those used in writing to argue; these two types of writing are closely linked.

- **Positive opening statement** to grab the audience's attention and to clearly state your opinion.
- **Evidence and justification** (e.g. this happened because…) give structure and reasoning to your opinion (use the PEE technique).
- Logical **connectives** to connect ideas and give structure to the piece.
- **Positive or negative vocabulary** at appropriate points to influence the audience's opinion.
- **Repetition** to emphasise your main points and make sure the audience has grasped the point.
- **Rhetorical questions** force the audience to question the issue – and its probable answer.

Rhetorical questions also make the audience feel more involved, as the question structure reflects speech, in which case the other person would be expected to be involved by providing an answer.

- **Formal tone** to make your opinion seem more credible.
- **Emotive language** to highlight the issues you are trying to persuade the audience about.
- **Comparative devices** such as similes and metaphors can emphasise your main points, often by attaching certain connotations.
- **Rule of three** is an effective way to stress a point.
- **Exaggeration** to grab the audience's attention and encourage them to be persuaded into accepting your opinion.
- **Personal pronouns** give a personal tone to the issue and make the audience feel more involved. Use of personal pronouns helps to establish a relationship between the writer and the audience.
- **Present tense** will make the issue seem more immediate and may therefore have the effect of pressurising the audience into being persuaded.
- **Conditional sentences** are effective as they express cause and effect, therefore suggesting what could happen if the audience does not agree.
- A **clear conclusion** that links to the introduction and summarises the main points in your piece of writing.

Look at the following example of writing to persuade. It is a letter, written by a teenager, to persuade her mother to allow her to go to a party.
(In the exam you will be expected to write more than this.)

This letter has been carefully crafted. It covers most of the techniques expected from this form of writing. Informal writing is difficult because you need to retain a level of formality. Remember that in the exam the examiner will be looking for evidence of **conscious crafting**. Conscious means that you have thought carefully about what you are writing, and crafting means that you have structured your work.

Exam Practice

Q. Write a leaflet to **persuade** the students at your school to take part in a 5km fun run to raise money for your favourite charity.

Personal pronouns

Positive opening statement

Present tense

Logical connectives

Conditional sentences

Emotive language

Comparative device – metaphor

Repetition, rule of three, rhetorical questions and parallelism

Positive and negative vocabulary

Rule of three

Exaggeration

Dear Mum,

You know how much I love you and I am writing this letter to let you know my reasons for wanting to go to the party on Friday night. I don't want to fall out with you so I thought I would put my feelings down for you to read in your own time. Once you have read my letter I will then accept whatever decision you make.

Firstly, this party on Friday night will be enjoyable, relaxing and fun for me: there will even be live music and dancing. I really want to go but I appreciate your concern that it is in the middle of exams. I thought we could compromise here: if I promise to work extra hard and produce a revision timetable which I will stick to, please will you let me go? I will make sure that every topic has been covered and I will give up going to the Youth Club for an entire month.

Moreover, studies say that you should revise in short bursts and reward yourself. I think this party will be the perfect opportunity to relax and can also be a reward that I can work towards. In fact, going to this party might even help me to improve my chances of success in the exams.

I know that you have my best interests at heart and want me to do well, but you seem to forget that I want that too. You must realise that I have high expectations of myself too, and won't let myself down. As you already know, I have been working incredibly hard since Christmas and am not about to fall at the last hurdle.

Finally, everyone I know will be going to this party. Surely you don't want me to be a social outcast? Surely you don't want me to be the only one who isn't there? Surely you don't want me to be miserable and lonely at this crucial time in my life? Mum, I beg you, please let your loving daughter go out on Friday night!

Love Jessica.

P.S. I promise to wash up for a month if you let me go.

Writing to Advise

Writing to advise means you taking on the role of the expert, as you will be telling someone else the best, easiest or quickest way to do something. The following points show the main things to remember when you are writing to advise. Covering these points in your writing will make your advice seem more professional and convincing.

A – Advice must be clear
D – Do keep in role
V – Vocabulary should include modal verbs
I – Informal but polite, use Imperatives
C – Choices must be given
E – Encourage and motivate

- **Advice must be clear**
  - You need to follow these three steps…
  - The first thing to do is…
- **Do keep in role**
  - It is my professional opinion that…
  - Many young people come to me for advice…
- **Vocabulary should include modal verbs**
  - can, will, shall, may, could, would, should, might, must, ought to.
- **Informal but polite**
  - Get your friends to help you…
  - Good luck…
  - Don't panic…
- **Choices must be given**
  - You must talk to your parents or another adult…
  - Alternatively…
  - If this doesn't work then…
- **Encourage and motivate**
  - Things may seem bad but don't worry…
  - You can be successful if you…

Language Techniques

- **Striking opening** to grab the audience's attention.
- Appropriate **connectives** to give your piece structure and to link your advice.
- **Modal verbs** to politely offer advice and choices in the form of suggestions. Modal verbs help to avoid a patronising tone in a piece of writing.
- **Informal tone** but polite, to establish respect and trust between the writer and the audience.
- **Positive vocabulary** to attract and interest the audience.
- **Comparative devices** to highlight points and to suggest the effectiveness of the advice.
- **Repetition** to emphasise the main points of the advice and to ensure the audience fully understands.
- **Imperatives** to give clear and straightforward advice / instruction.
- **First and second person pronouns** to maintain a relationship between the writer and the audience, and to signify the role of the expert.
- **Questions** to involve the audience and hold their interest.
- **Bullet points** to organise the advice so that it can be followed easily.
- **Exclamations** to add a lively tone to the writing.
- **Conditional sentences** are effective as they express cause and effect, therefore suggesting what could / could not happen as a result of following / not following the advice given.
- **Concluding paragraph** to summarise the advice and / or give a positive message.

The first thing to do is...

Look at the following piece of writing which offers advice to students on how to deal with exam stress. (In the exam you will be expected to write more than this.)

This piece of writing gives clear advice in an informal but polite tone. The writer remains in role as the expert throughout, and uses language which encourages and motivates.

Exam Practice

Q. Imagine you are an agony aunt for a teenagers' magazine. Respond to a letter from a 14 year-old girl whose friends are pressurising her into taking up smoking. She doesn't want to smoke and needs your **advice** on how to keep her friends without giving in to peer pressure.

Modal verbs

Repetition and parallelism

First and second person pronouns

Questions

Conditional sentences

Suitable connectives

Imperatives

Informal tone

Exclamations

Rhyme

Do you feel you have a lot to revise but no time to do it?
Do you feel you can't take in all the information?
Do you feel blank when you read your notes?

If you answered 'yes' to any of the above, you may be suffering from stress. Stress is natural, but you can learn how to manage it. By following the tips below, you can drastically reduce the levels of stress you experience and, whilst we can't guarantee to completely eradicate stress, we can help you to manage the stress you are feeling. Follow our top ten tension-busting tips.

1. **Learn to relax.**
   This could mean taking a long bath, watching television, or even listening to relaxation tapes. Whatever you do, be sure to make time for relaxation.

2. **Get organised.**
   Draw up a realistic schedule of daily activities that you can focus on and achieve. The key here is to remember pace not race: it is far more effective to work surely and steadily.

3. **Exercise.**
   Exercise is a fabulous stress buster. Take time out every day to exercise, even if it is just a short walk.

4. **Talk.**
   Talking to family or friends can stop you worrying. Remember your friends are in the same situation and will understand.

5. **Make a list.**
   Write down all the things that are worrying you and get someone you trust to go through them with you. Remember, a problem shared is a problem halved.

6. **Think positively.**
   Make sure you are in a calm and positive mood before you start to study. Deep breathing and meditation should help to focus your mind.

7. **Sleep.**
   Being tired doesn't help anyone. Your brain needs time to relax in order to function effectively. Ensure that you get plenty of sleep during the important revision period.

8. **Eat sensibly.**
   You should eat a healthy, balanced diet. Omega 3 oils (found in oily fish) and thiamine (found in wholemeal bread) help the brain to function at its best.

9. **Drink water.**
   Dehydration can make you feel tired and sluggish. Drinking plenty of water will ensure that you are properly hydrated and will make you think more clearly.

10. **Be confident.**
    Why wouldn't you do well? If you believe in yourself, you will do well.

At the end of the day, no one likes exams but they are something we all have to do. Just remember, the optimism of action is better than the pessimism of thought!

Exam Tips

Useful Words and Phrases

There are certain words and phrases that can be very useful in writing to argue, persuade or advise. A / A* candidates should be able to demonstrate the use of such words and phrases in their writing in a natural and fluent manner. Some of these words and phrases are given here with descriptions of how and when you should use them.

- **To state your opinions:** these phrases indicate that what follows is your personal opinion. They are polite and quite formal, and are therefore useful in letters and speeches etc.
  – I feel / think / consider…
  – In my opinion…
  – I am convinced that…
- **To link your ideas / opinions:** these connectives (see page 35) make your writing flow well.
  – In addition…
  – A further consideration must be…
  – Similarly…

- **To introduce evidence:** these phrases can be useful in backing up your idea or opinion.
  – It has come to my attention that…
  – A recent survey in the newspaper found that…
- **To give the alternative view:** these phrases help to justify your opinion by implying that other people have the same opinion as you.
  – Some people have said that…
  – Some people believe that…
  – Many people think…
- **To present a balanced view:** these connectives suggest that a new idea / opinion will follow. They are used when one idea / opinion has been discussed, and a new one is being introduced.
  – However…
  – On the other hand…
  – Nevertheless…
- **To be convincing (but polite):** these phrases show that you accept other opinions can be valid.
  – Clearly some people will have opposing views, but I believe…
  – I understand your objections…
  – I am sure you will agree that…
- **To discredit the other opinion:** these phrases suggest that there is evidence to prove that the other opinion / idea is wrong and that an explanation will follow to say why it is wrong.
  – Clearly, this is not true…
  – However, this is not the case…
  – This is misleading…

Checking Your Work

You should spend five minutes of your time checking your answer. It is easy to make mistakes with spelling, punctuation and grammar so it is important to read through your answer carefully when you have finished it. Make sure you have…

- used paragraphs
- linked your paragraphs with suitable connectives
- used a variety of punctuation correctly and appropriately (including apostrophes, commas, colons, semi-colons etc.)
- used a variety of sentence structures
- spelt words correctly
- crossed out any mistakes neatly and written your corrections so that the examiner can clearly understand your intentions.

Paper 2

Section A

48   Reading Poetry from Different Cultures

Section B

72   Writing to Inform, Explain or Describe

Reading Poetry from Different Cultures

The Exam Question

Section A of Paper 2 tests your knowledge and in-depth understanding of poetry from different cultures. You will have already read the poems and made notes in your anthology, but to get the highest grades you need to produce an original and engaged response to the poems. In the exam you will have a clean copy of the anthology so you won't have your notes. You need to read the poems thoroughly and make some original observations before the exam. Do not rely on revision notes; try to come up with some original ideas and observations of your own.

You will have a choice of two questions which will ask you to compare two or more poems in terms of culture and traditions. You will have 45 minutes to answer **one** of these questions. Plan your answer before you begin and make sure everything you write is relevant to the question.

What is the examiner looking for?

The examiner wants to see that you can read, understand and compare poems. To achieve a grade A or A* you must show that you can do the following.

- Refer in detail to aspects of language, structure and presentation – close textual analysis.
- Comment in detail on stylistic features and the effects that they produce.
- Comment on any presentational devices that are used (e.g. font sizes, the layout of the words on the page, the length, order and structure of the stanzas).
- Comment on the use of contrast by the poets.
- Select appropriate material to support your answer, making cross-references where appropriate.

- Use relevant quotes from the poems. Your references should be integrated into your response.
- Make suitable and careful comparisons and contrasts within and between the poems.
- Describe how style can change throughout a poem.
- Explore and empathise with the writers' ideas and attitudes through consistent insight and convincing and imaginative interpretation.

The PEE Technique

Always use the 'PEE' technique (you must have a three-part response to your answers):

P   Make a **P**oint
E   Use **E**vidence from the poem (a quote)
E   Give an **E**xplanation to back up the point. Explain why the evidence illustrates your point.

For example:

Point: The salwar kameez that is sent to the girl in the poem *Presents from My Aunts in Pakistan* is beautiful.

Evidence: It is described as 'glistening like an orange split open'.

Explanation: This simile portrays its shining beauty and yet, whilst the girl can appreciate its splendour, she would rather wear a pair of jeans. She feels that she cannot be as beautiful as the clothes that she is sent.

Examiner's Tips

Plan your answer carefully. Make sure you write about the poems that are best suited to the question, rather than just writing about your favourite poems. Make your own personal observations about the poems and support your observations with PEE.

Culture and Traditions

▮ What are culture and traditions?

You will be familiar with the terms **culture** and **traditions**. All the poems that you have studied in the anthology cover aspects of different cultures and traditions. You should have thought about the ways in which the poems portray aspects of these concepts. The ways that the writers use language in their poems to depict particular cultures and traditions indicate how they feel about them.

Culture is a person's background with reference to their language, their way of life and their beliefs. Traditions are associated with different cultures. They are customs that people of a particular culture uphold.

▮ Culture

Culture refers to...
- people's origins and backgrounds
- the language that people speak
- traditions that people uphold
- the way that people are expected to behave in a particular society
- the politics of a particular country or society
- people's beliefs and their religion.

▮ Traditions

Traditions refer to...
- the way that people behave in certain situations
- things that people say
- events, festivals and celebrations associated with a particular culture.

You need to have a clear idea of what these terms mean to enable you to write about them effectively in the exam.

It is important to avoid stereotyping through these terms. You will be writing about the people or the culture as portrayed in the poems that you have chosen to write about, not about *all* such people or similar cultures. Remember that 'different' is defined as being synonymous with 'other.'

Examiner's Tip

Do not be afraid to express your own opinions about the poems, but make sure that your comments are backed up with textual evidence.

Poetry Terms

The examiner wants to see that you are able to write about the poems from a range of perspectives. You must be able to describe each in terms of…

- **Content:** what the poem is about
- **Setting:** where and when the poem is set
- **Themes:** issues the writer wants to highlight and / or wants the reader to consider
- **Style:** the way that the writer uses words (diction), the effect that they have on the reader, and the impact that the writer intended them to have.

You are expected to be able to convey the full meanings of the poems on their various levels, and to be able to write fluently about the writers' use of style to create particular effects. Here is a reminder of the correct terms for the writers' techniques (see also pages 6–7):

- **Accent:** the way a character would sound if he / she spoke
- **Adjectives:** describe nouns
- **Adverbs:** describe verbs (the action)
- **Alliteration:** repetition of a sound at the beginning of words
- **Ambiguity:** having more than one meaning
- **Assonance:** rhyme of the internal vowel sound
- **Contrast:** a strong difference between two things
- **Connotations of words:** the meanings they suggest
- **Dialect:** non-standard use of words and grammar

- **Dialogue:** a conversation
- **Exclamations:** portray emotions
- **Elision:** one word runs into another
- **Enjambment:** lines run on and are not stopped at the end
- **Indentation:** writing away from the margin
- **Imagery:** the use of descriptive words to create a picture in the reader's mind
- **Irony and sarcasm:** the use of words to imply the opposite of their meaning
- **Juxtaposition:** the positioning of words / phrases / ideas close together for effect
- **Lineation:** arrangement in lines
- **Metaphor:** an image created by referring to something as something else
- **Onomatopoeia:** words that sound like their meaning
- **Oxymoron:** two contradictory terms together
- **Pathetic fallacy:** when the surroundings reflect the mood of the character
- **Personification:** giving an inanimate object animate (or human) qualities
- **Perspective:** a way of looking at something
- **Puns / play on words:** words used in an amusing way to suggest other meanings
- **Received Pronunciation:** a prestigious accent
- **Repetition:** words, phrases, sentences or structures repeated
- **Rhetorical questions:** questions that don't require answers: the answer is obvious
- **Rhyme:** the use of rhyming words to affect the sound pattern. End rhyme, full rhyme, internal rhyme
- **Rhythm:** the beat of the poem when read aloud
- **Sibilance:** alliteration with the 's' sound
- **Simile:** a comparison using 'as' or 'like'
- **Standard English:** the standard use of words and grammar
- **Symbolism:** represents an abstract idea
- **Tone:** the overall attitude of the poem.

Examiner's Tip

Use these terms to explain how the poets use language techniques to achieve particular effects, and the impact of these techniques on the reader.

The following pages (51–66) study the poems in the Anthology, with reference to content, setting, themes and style. Read the poems before and after reading the information in this guide.

Limbo Edward Kamau Brathwaite

Content

The poet uses the connotations of the word limbo to enhance the poem's three meanings: limbo the dance; limbo the place between heaven and hell; in limbo (stuck in the middle of two situations).

The poem is about slaves being brought from Africa to America, and the hardships they endured. It describes the African limbo dance being performed; the stick is continually lowered so it is increasingly difficult to get beneath it, which could reflect the poet's ideas about the slaves' situation. The African people were beaten to the ground and subjugated to the will of their owners, leading them into limbo of the third kind: trapped between their backgrounds of freedom, and their new lives as slaves.

Setting

Africa is evoked through phrases like 'sun coming up' and 'burning ground'. The slave ship's deck is referred to as 'long dark deck' which evokes images of hell.

Themes

The themes are echoed through the title of the poem.

- People being in limbo (trapped in two situations).
- The survival of ancient traditions (the limbo dance).
- Slavery and corruption, and the subjugation of human beings to the will of others.
- The strength of the spirit and free will, enabling people to survive in ill-fated circumstances.
- The clash of cultures: the slaves and their masters had different languages, resulting in a 'silence' between them.
- The endurance of people and the sustainability of their cultures.

Style

- **Alliteration** stresses words that describe the deck of the slave ship and its multiplicity of meanings.
- Strong **rhythm** and **rhyme** echo the limbo music. The disjointed pattern reflects the disjointed lives the slaves were forced to lead – trapped between two cultures.
- **Enjambment** enables the lines to run on, reflecting the slaves' situation (and the limbo dance).
- **Symbolism:** the stick is a symbol of oppression: the character gets lower to the ground and closer to being a total slave. At times the stick is a whip with which the slaves are beaten.
- **Imagery:** the image of rape is evident: 'knees spread wide'. The physical force into the ground represents the domination of the slaves. Images of darkness, oppression and violence pervade the beginning of the poem.
- **Repetition** of 'limbo like me' makes the reader consider its meanings, and suggests that the suffering is ongoing.
- **Negative diction**, e.g. 'dark', 'silence', stresses the loneliness and despair of being in captivity.
- By line 40 more **positive images** enter the poem: the sun symbolises a bright new life, and 'raising me' and 'saving me' suggest hope. However, the burning ground at the end of the poem could also allude to the images of hell found earlier in the poem; have the people entered a new hell?
- The poem is written from a **personal perspective** making it seem more genuine.
- The use of the **present tense** suggests that oppression is ongoing.

Nothing's Changed Tatamkhulu Afrika

Content

The poem is about a man's journey to a district that has changed in recent years. It takes him back to his childhood and, although superficially things have changed, the ingrained race divisions still remain.

The area is District Six, an area for whites only during apartheid. Now anybody can go there. It is being redeveloped and now houses expensive restaurants. However, at the time the poem was written, many black people in South Africa would not have been able to afford to go there, nor would they feel welcome which angers the poet (as can be seen in the final lines with their undertone of violence). It is as if apartheid still exists in the country, even though legally it was abolished in the early 1990s.

Setting

The poem is set in District Six, an area in Cape Town, South Africa, that was declared for whites only during apartheid (1964), leading to the eviction of thousands of black and mixed-race citizens. The area is one of contrast: the upper-class restaurant with linen table cloths and single roses on the tables, and the working man's café down the road characterised by local food, plastic tables and spit on the floor. The setting represents the differences in the living standards of some communities in South Africa, even today.

Themes

- Apartheid: its impact on South Africa and its people.
- Racial discrimination.

- Anger and frustration caused by social injustice.
- Alienation and exclusion from society: '…we know where we belong.'
- The impact of childhood memories; they remain with us and shape our politics and personalities.

Style

- **Symbolism:** District Six (the most famous community from which black and mixed-race citizens were evicted) represents apartheid. The glass in the window represents the racial divide and the barriers that still remain despite the fact that apartheid has been abolished.
- **Assonance**, e.g. 'ice white' and 'spit a little', is used to stress the character's anger.
- **Alliteration** of the harsh 'c' sound, e.g. 'into trouser cuffs, cans', expresses the poet's resentment.
- **Angry diction** conveys how the poet is feeling, e.g. 'mean mouth', 'a bomb, to shiver down the glass'.
- **Enjambment:** the lines run on allowing the reader to follow the character's journey physically and mentally.
- **Synonyms of intrusion**, e.g. 'thrust', 'press', which raises the question of who the intruders are – the black or white communities?
- **Onomatopoeia**, e.g. 'click', 'crunch,' 'spit', helps us to follow the man on his journey through the district, literally and metaphorically.
- **Circular structure:** the title is repeated at the end to show that 'Nothing's changed'.
- The poem is written as a **first person account** which makes us empathise with the man's situation and the feelings that his experiences evoke.

Island Man Grace Nichols

Content

The poem recounts the character waking up one morning in London. He once lived on a Caribbean island and still wakes up every morning to the sounds and happy memories of the Caribbean. The Caribbean morning that he thinks he has awoken to contrasts sharply with the reality of his life in London.

Setting

The poem is set in London, near the 'dull North circular' road, but the place that is described beautifully is the island in the Caribbean. The juxtaposition of the two descriptions enables the comparison between them to be highlighted effectively.

Themes

- Separation: the man yearns for his home on the Caribbean island.
- Alienation and loneliness.
- Love of your homeland: we know that the man thinks favourably about his homeland through the diction used to describe it.
- Imagination and reality.
- The impact of childhood on our lives: the man's fond memories of the island on which he grew up.

Style

- **Imagery:** the words used help us to picture the Caribbean island. The language appeals to the senses (sight, sound, touch): we can 'hear' the waves crashing on the beach, and the sound of the gulls.
- **Adjectives** and **adverbs** enable the reader to picture the scenes vividly and empathise with the character.
- The poem is written from an **impersonal perspective** (third person, 'island man'), which emphasises the character's detachment from his life.
- **Contrast** and **juxtaposition** of the beautiful Caribbean island ('emerald island') with the busy London road ('North Circular roar'). The 'blue surf' contrasts with the 'grey metallic soar' of London.
- **Duality of meaning:** 'wombing' (a reference to the womb) indicates the richness of the sea and the life it contains, and stresses the fact that the man was born in the Caribbean.
- **Repetition** and **alliteration**, e.g. 'groggily, groggily' stress the man's feelings in the poem. This adverb stresses that he is disappointed when he remembers the reality of his situation.
- **Effective use of verbs**, e.g. 'heaves', shows that the man is reluctant to face the reality of his day in London.
- **Sibilance:** the 'sound of the blue surf', appeals to our senses by echoing the sound of the sea.
- The **absence of punctuation** allows the poem to flow, giving it a dream-like quality.
- Use of the **present tense**: both situations are a reality for the character – he lives them both at once. He has not assigned his island home to the past; it is still very much part of his life.

Blessing Imtiaz Dharker

Content

The poem depicts the scene in an Indian village when a water pipe bursts unexpectedly. The children play in the water and the people collect water in anything they can find. The poem portrays what a precious commodity water is in some places around the world.

Setting

The poem is set in an Indian village that has been suffering from drought. The 'skin' (soil) of the village 'cracks like a pod' when the water pipe bursts. The scene is described vividly; the people rush around the village, and the children play in the 'liquid sun'.

Themes

- The simplicity of life in many villages around the world: the people in the poem have basic needs. They value water ('the blessing'), something that other societies take for granted.
- The power of nature: water can transform a scene and the lives of the people in it.
- The daily struggle to survive in developing countries: the children are having fun but the poem refers to their 'small bones', reminding us that they are weak and undernourished. We are also told at the beginning, 'there never is enough water'. The poet makes us consider how blessings can be different things to different people.

Style

- **Positive diction**, e.g. 'kindly', 'silver', 'sun', 'polished to perfection', emphasises what a blessing the water is for the community.
- **Appealing to the senses:** we can picture the scene through the images and 'hear' the effects of the water through the use of **onomatopoeia**, e.g. 'splash', 'rush', 'crashes'.
- **Short lines and phrases** echo the drops of water.
- **Similes**, e.g. 'the skin cracks like a pod'; this describes how dry the land is. The image created makes the scene more vivid for the reader.
- **Metaphors:** the sound of the water is so good that it sounds like 'the voice of a kindly god'. **Personification** is used in this metaphor. The water is given human (in fact superhuman) qualities and appreciated as something special.
- Religious **imagery**, e.g. the phrase 'a roar of tongues' reminds us of a choir singing. The people are referred to as a 'congregation' which is what we call a group of people in church, and the title of the poem 'Blessing' is a part of church services. The poet creates a photographic portrayal of the village through sustained use of imagery.
- **Enjambment:** the lines unfold and flood the page, as the scene unfolds before the reader.
- The wondrous scene is **juxtaposed** with the political reality that some communities lack basic commodities like water. The poem begins and ends with these realities.

Content

The poem describes two garbage men in their garbage truck waiting at some traffic lights alongside a glamorous young couple in a Mercedes. The two vehicles and their occupants could not be more different, reflecting that on a deeper level the poem is about injustice in societies. It questions whether America is really a democracy and whether it is really the land of opportunity for all.

Setting

The poem is set in San Francisco, America.

Themes

- Social injustice: in some societies there seem to be two social groups – the couple in the car and the garbage men represent these groups. The easy lifestyle of the wealthy (the architect in his Mercedes) contrasts with the hard life of the garbage men who have been clinging to the back of the garbage truck since four in the morning.

- America is often referred to as the 'land of dreams' where people can be whatever they want to be, but here the poet suggests that this is not true. The garbage men watch the couple as if watching a television advert where people are able to do anything they want. The reference to a television advert reinforces that this idea is not a reality for them.

- Political protest: is America really the land of opportunity? Although both sets of people work, their jobs and lifestyles are very different.

Style

- The poem has a **narrative** quality: the poet is a social commentator on the scene he describes. The language is simple and direct, and the **lack of punctuation** allows the scene to unfold without interruption, culminating in the freeze frame of the two couples at the traffic lights.

- **Contrast** is used effectively throughout the poem to stress the differences between the characters, physically and socially. Contrast begins in the poem's title with 'scavengers' and 'beautiful', 'truck' and 'Mercedes'. The two couples are **juxtaposed** throughout the poem to highlight the contrast between them.

- **Repetition:** certain phrases are repeated in slightly different forms in lines 30 and 33 to show that the poet does not believe this is true and wants the reader to consider the idea carefully.

- **Alliteration** stresses key points about the characters.

- **Adjectives** paint the scene vividly in the reader's mind.

- **Similes:** the garbage man is described as a gargoyle and Quasimodo: ugly creatures.

- The **layout** is unusual and therefore highlights the unusual social situation that the poet is describing.

- **Extended image** of a journey: the Mercedes, the garbage truck and the reference to the sea. The poet could be suggesting that life is a journey and we all reach different destinations.

Examiner's Tip

You can use shortened versions of the poems' titles in the exam (e.g. 'Two Scavengers'), as long as it is clear which poem you are referring to.

Night of the Scorpion Nissim Ezekiel

Content

The poet vividly describes a night in his village when he was a little boy and his mother was stung by a scorpion. All the villagers came to help in her recovery. His father was worried and, although he was normally a very rational man, he tried all sorts of strange remedies such as putting paraffin on the sting and lighting it. The holy man also performed some rituals to try to cure her. His mother recovers and is just glad that the scorpion stung her and not one of her children.

Setting

The poem is set in a village in India; everywhere is drenched following torrential rain. The primitive village is described in detail by the poet's series of snapshots of the night which focus on the neighbours and their behaviour, their huts and the holy man who comes to help. The descriptions depict the culture in great detail.

Themes

- The selfless love that mothers have for their children.
- The closeness of some communities; everyone came out to help, showing real community spirit.
- The strength of childhood memories: the poet remembers the night in great detail.

Style

- The poem has a **narrative** quality; it is written in free verse and reads like a story.
- The poem is written in the **first person**, enabling the reader to engage in the story that unfolds.
- **Imagery:** the idea that the scorpion is the devil runs throughout: the words 'evil' and 'diabolic' are used in reference to it. This also reflects the superstitious beliefs of the villagers.
- **Rhythm:** the rhythm of the lines echo normal speech so we feel we are listening to a story unfolding.
- **Similes:** the peasants are compared to flies, suggesting there are many of them dashing around making a cacophony of noise.
- **Repetition** of 'may…'. The chants are used by the villagers, reflecting their superstitious beliefs. The holy man is sent for, not a doctor as we would expect in our society.
- **Negative diction** is used to emphasise his mother's pain, e.g. 'groaning'.
- **Adjectives** add to the vivid and detailed description of life in the village.
- **Alliteration** stresses the negative things that occur throughout the poem.

Vultures Chinua Achebe

Content

On the surface, the poem describes two vultures in a tree. The previous day, they ate the innards of a dead animal; today they are observed being affectionate with one another, highlighting how love and brutality can co-exist. The poem emphasises this by describing a commandant in a German concentration camp who is involved in the burning of the Jews but, on his way home, he thoughtfully stops to buy chocolate for his children.

The poet is stating that there can be goodness in the most evil heart and vice versa. He explores the concept of evil, concluding that it is difficult to define.

Setting

The poem is set on the plains of Nigeria and in the concentration camps of Nazi Germany. The diversity of these settings reinforces the point that evil can be found in a multitude of places.

Themes

- The duality (two sides) of life.
- The many facets (sides) of the human heart.
- The contrast between nature and human nature and the motivation behind our actions: the vultures eat the dead animal to survive; the camp commandant kills people because he is ordered to do so.
- The constant presence of evil; it will always endure.
- The deceptive nature of appearances – it is not wise to take things at face value.

Style

- The lines are irregular in length and there is no regular rhyme scheme. This helps to reinforce that nature and human beings are unpredictable.
- **Enjambment** emphasises the continuation of evil.
- **Irony:** it is a sad irony that the commandant is part of the cruel process of gassing the Jewish people, but he has the kindness to stop and buy chocolate for his children.
- **Contrast:** the poem opens with **bleak diction**, e.g. 'greyness' and 'drizzle', yet the vultures lean towards each other 'affectionately'. The commandant goes home with the smell of 'human roast clinging' to his nostrils, but he goes home to his 'tender offspring'. This contrast stresses the theme of duality. The poem alternates between **positive and negative diction**.
- **Juxtaposition** of positive and negative diction reinforces the multi-faceted nature of things, as does the juxtaposition of the descriptions of the vultures and the commandant.
- **Alliteration** is used throughout the poem to stress key concepts that the poet wants us to consider, such as the 'icy caverns of a cruel heart'.
- **Metaphors**, e.g. 'a pebble on a stem…'. This metaphor stresses the ugliness of the vultures.
- The **metaphor** on lines 44–47 describes tenderness in 'icy caverns of a cruel heart'. This seems to indicate the continuous nature of the dichotomy (two parts) presented in the poem.
- **Religious diction** is used to suggest that even the most repulsive things in life do have some goodness in them. The poet is expressing that we should be grateful for all the positive things that we find in life.

What Were They Like? Denise Levertov

Content

The poem consists of a series of numbered questions and answers about the Vietnamese war which lasted from 1954 until 1975. The Americans intervened in the war, although many thought they should not have done so as it was a civil war. There were many atrocities on both sides throughout its duration.

The poem describes what the Vietnamese people were like before the war, how they lived contentedly in a civilisation characterised by beautiful art and culture, living simply and working in the rice fields. Then the war changed everything, and its effect on the country is documented.

Setting

The soldier describes Vietnam in South East Asia before and after the war. It is suggested that before the war Vietnam was a beautiful and tranquil place with lanterns lighting the paths, and pretty blossoms. In the aftermath it was filled with charred bones, dead children, and silent, bombed fields.

Themes

- The atrocities of war: how people's lives can be destroyed.
- Celebration of another culture: the diction used portrays Vietnam before the war as a beautiful place with content people.

Style

- The poem is laid out as a set of **questions** in the first stanza, which are answered in the second (probably by a soldier, as 'Sir' is used).
- In the first stanza the language is conversational in tone and direct in style.
- The first stanza highlights the positive qualities of the country. It is harshly answered in stanza two with a **metaphor** which stresses the extent to which the people's lives were changed by war.
- The second stanza is full of poetic phrases as it describes the place before the war with its people whose 'speech… was like a song'. The **sibilance** stresses the positive qualities of the Vietnamese.
- **Alliteration** with the soft 'm' sound, 'moths in moonlight' emphasises the peace and quiet of the country prior to the war.
- **Interrogatives** are used to make the reader consider particular subjects. The soldier is being asked the questions, but so too are the readers of the poem. The title itself sets this tone.
- **Violent diction** and **images** are used throughout the poem to show the poet's disapproval of the war – 'hearts turned to stone,' 'bitter to the burned mouth' (describes people who had their mouths burned by the napalm bombs), 'bombs smashed those mirrors' and 'time only to scream'.
- **Positive diction** is applied to the place and people before the war, e.g. 'pleasant ways,' and 'delight in blossom'.
- **Contrast** is used effectively in the poem to stress what the country was like before and after the war. This enables the tone of the poem to imply the poet's disapproval of the war.

(From) Search for My Tongue Sujata Bhatt

Content

The persona (character) is expressing how difficult it is to be bilingual as you are never sure which language to use and, as a result, end up questioning your own sense of identity. She points out that it is difficult to be part of two cultures as you are unsure which culture you really belong to. She has a dream where her mother tongue (the language she grew up speaking) grows in her mouth like a flower. This part of the poem is written in Gujarati, her mother tongue. The dream metaphorically represents the ever-present blossoming of her mother tongue over her second language, and this defines her real self.

Setting

The poem does not have an obvious setting; it is in the woman's thoughts. Her mouth becomes the setting, in her dream, as it turns into a growing garden.

Themes

- Cultural identity: belonging to two different cultures and the inherent problems this brings.
- Belonging: the need for people to fit in with certain groups to provide a sense of identity.
- The importance of language: it defines us as people and is part of our cultural and personal identity.

Style

- The **first person** ('me', 'I') is used to create a very personal opening and address.
- The **questioning** at the opening of the poem reflects the fact that the woman is questioning herself about her cultural identity and the importance of her language in defining herself.
- The start of the poem is **conversational in tone**.
- An **image** of the woman's mother tongue as a growing, living thing runs through the poem from line 12. It is given a **positive significance**, as it is referred to as blossom. The word blossom denotes a growing, beautiful, vibrant entity.
- The section that deals with the difficulty of speaking two languages has **harsh diction**, e.g. 'rot', 'die' and 'spit'. The **synonyms** denote death and destruction. The **repetition** of these words ('rot' and 'spit') also emphasises the frustration and anger she feels.

- **Assonance**, e.g. on lines 13 ('mouth') and 14 ('out') is used to stress the negative diction.
- The **Gujarati** stands out in the poem, showing its importance in her life. It leaps off the page just like it leaps out of her mouth. It describes the language flowering in her mouth as she is asleep, and is full of **positive diction**.
- **Metaphors:** the idea of the woman's mother tongue as a bud (a growing thing) runs throughout the poem.
- **Repetition** is used effectively to emphasise how she repeats the dilemma to herself and tries to come to terms with it.

(From) Unrelated Incidents Tom Leonard

Content

The poem is about attitudes towards non-standard accents and dialects and how we are characterised by the way that we speak. It is written as a phonetic (written as it sounds) transcript of a Glaswegian accent in the form of a television autocue. The character in the poem is pretending to be a newsreader to make the point that just because he does not use Standard English (as newsreaders do) it does not mean that he is not trustworthy or worthy of respect. He is commenting on the snobbery associated with accents, and challenging the presumptions people make about others based on their accents.

Setting

An internalised setting – the man's thoughts, set out to look like an autocue in a television studio.

Themes

- Standard English and Received Pronunciation are regarded as the dialect and accent of status and authority.
- Social identity and cultural identity: the man belongs to a particular social group and he uses the language of that group. However, he is aware that some people patronise him and might make false assumptions about him due to the way that he speaks.

- Injustice and prejudice in society: the poet states that people are judged by the language they use. He says that people might think he is a 'scruff' because of his accent.
- The truth: the poem challenges what we mean by the truth. The truth can be different things to different people. He thinks that all accents are equal; this is his truth, but others would not agree.

Style

- **Dialectal words and phrases** are used throughout the poem, e.g. 'belt up', 'coz', and 'scruff'. They are used to show to which social group the persona belongs. He values the way that he speaks and feels that it is good enough to use in his poem.
- The poem starts with language that is close to **Standard English** but it becomes more dialectal as it progresses.
- The poet concludes with the rather aggressive phrase 'belt up', expressing his anger with people who look down on non-standard accents.
- The **layout** is unusual, comprising short phrases. It looks like a television autocue from which newsreaders read. This highlights the **contrast** between the **accent** and **dialect** used by newsreaders, and the strong Scottish accent and non-standard dialect used by the character in the poem.

Half-Caste John Agard

Content

The poem is an objection to the term 'half-caste' used to mean 'of mixed race'. The poet objects to the use of the word 'half' because half of something implies that it is inferior to the whole thing. Therefore, 'half-caste' implies that people of mixed race are inferior. Although the poem treats the topic with some humour, the underlying anger at the situation is always apparent.

Setting

The poem is set as though the poet is speaking to people who use the term 'half-caste', an English language term which means the poet is referring to English-speaking societies. The setting is society in general, but it does refer to the weather in England, suggesting that the poet may be referring more specifically to English society.

Themes

- The problem of applying a term to a group of people as it can cause offence.
- Racial prejudice: some people have different views of people who have different coloured skin to their own, and treat them differently.
- The use of language to define your cultural, social and personal identity.
- The inequalities that can be encouraged by defining people through certain language, and the resentment that this can create.

Style

- The introduction to the poem is like a greeting and 'excuse me' is used **sarcastically** by the character to apologise for being different.
- The poem is a dramatic **monologue** (a piece that could be performed on stage). Monologues are often used to make comments about society as they are quite direct in tone and use the second person ('you'). Punctuation often is not used because it is supposed to sound like speech, which is not punctuated. Alternatively, it could be seen as a challenge to grammatical conventions just as the poet is challenging society's views.
- The poem is written in the **first person** so the reader can empathise with the character's feelings.
- It is written in a Caribbean **dialect**, which is a form of **Creole** (a language or dialect based on two or more languages). This shows that the poet values this form of language; he uses it to mock the attitudes of people who call him 'half-caste'.
- The poem presents the reader with a series of funny **images**, e.g. standing on 'one leg'. This **humorous** tone shows that the poet does not take the people who term him half-caste seriously. He tells them to open their minds and use their whole brain to see him for what he is – a human being.
- The poet wishes people could see with their 'whole' eye (line 48). This **metaphoric phrase** means he wishes people could see things as they really are.
- **Repetition** of the word 'half', and the many different contexts the poet puts it into, emphasises the stupidity of using the term 'half-caste'.

Love After Love Derek Walcott

Content

The poem is about self-discovery – learning, accepting and celebrating who you are, and valuing all the things that have been instrumental in shaping you. It describes how we often ignore our own emotional needs in order to give attention to other people, but we should make time for ourselves and value our own lives. The poet values his past and all the experiences that have made him who he is today, even the painful experiences.

Setting

The poem is set in a metaphorical house which represents the internal thoughts of the writer. It is set in our own past, present and future. It is a theoretical setting.

Themes

- The value of the past in helping to shape you into the person that you become with time and experience.
- The importance of your background and the things that you have experienced in life.
- The importance of being comfortable and happy with who you are; the acceptance of who you are. This is a universal theme, related to all mankind, not just to one social or cultural group.

Style

- There is a series of **metaphors** in the poem: the mirror is the way we see ourselves and look back at the past; 'feast on your life' makes life seem like a delicious banquet which should be enjoyed to the full; and the person who is greeted at the door is our old self (how we used to be).
- The **extended metaphor** of the body being a house runs throughout the poem.
- **Religious diction** is used, e.g. 'Give wine. Give bread'. These words are part of religious services and give a formal, sincere and caring tone to the poem. They stress that we should appreciate our past as it shapes our future and who we will become.
- The ideas in the poem are complex, but the language used is very simple.
- The poem reads like a series of **instructions** (**imperatives**) on how to accept yourself for what you are, and rejoice in what you find.
- **Enjambment:** the lines run on which reinforces the point that our lives are a series of events that run together to shape us into what we will become.

This Room Imtiaz Dharker

Content

Like other poems (e.g. *Limbo, Two Scavengers*), the poem exists on more than one level. Superficially, it describes a room that has gone wild; all the items in it are trying to escape. They are in search of 'space, light and empty air' which symbolically represent freedom. On a deeper level, the room is the metaphor used to describe the person in the poem who feels that it is time to break away from the predictable and the restraints that society places on people. The character is given the chance to do this 'when the improbable arrives'. The poet is saying that we should welcome times like this and use them as a chance to escape from the way that things have been in the past.

The poem celebrates the fact that life is unpredictable and exciting. The reader can feel the excitement through the images that are used.

Setting

The poem is set in a metaphorical house, from which the rooms and their contents are trying to escape. It is also an internalised setting – the woman's thought processes as she thinks about her life and the person that she has become.

Themes

- Celebration of the fact that life can be unpredictable.
- Celebration of personal growth and life.
- The fact that change can be a good, exciting thing, not something to worry about.
- Freedom: freedom is the most important element in our lives and we should make the most of it.
- Identity: identity comes from a state of mind not nationality or religion.

Style

- The poem is written in **free verse** (no structure to the verses) which helps to convey the message that nothing is more valuable than our freedom.
- The poem is full of movement, which is reinforced by the use of **enjambment**.
- **Personification:** the room is portrayed as a person who is full of energy.
- **Imagery:** the pots, pans and the bed are images used to represent the quest for freedom.

- **Present participle:** the verbs are in the -ing form (e.g. 'breaking', 'clapping', 'lifting'), which adds immediacy. This enables the reader to get involved in the action and enhances the idea that what is currently happening in our lives is important and will shape what we become in the future.
- **Alliteration**, e.g. 'corners…crash through the clouds'. The harsh sounds compliment the idea of breaking out and escaping.
- **Onomatopoeia** is used to enhance the sound effects of the poem. You can 'hear' some of the words, e.g. 'cracking', 'crash', and 'clang'.
- The poem appeals to the **senses** to emphasise the pleasure of being alive and free.

Not My Business · Niyi Osundare

Content

The poem is about the unfair treatment of citizens by the authorities, especially military regimes. It depicts a culture where the injustice of a regime becomes commonplace and people worry only about themselves. The poet describes how those who are not directly affected do not seem to care as long as they themselves are safe and have enough to eat. It also suggests that they feel powerless – they cannot do anything. In the final stanza the writer becomes the target of the injustice when the jeep that is used to take people away arrives at his house.

The poet is trying to convey the message that we cannot ignore injustice just because it does not affect us. It is short-sighted because, eventually, injustice affects everybody.

Setting

The poem is set in Nigeria, Africa: the characters' names are Nigerian and the poet was born in Nigeria.

Themes

- The inane brutality of military regimes.
- Injustice and inequality in society.
- Self-preservation: people often turn a blind eye to injustice if they are not directly affected. However, this situation can have disastrous consequences as corruption spreads through the whole of these societies and nobody is safe.
- Persecution of citizens by the authorities.

Style

- **Violent diction** is used throughout the poem, e.g. 'beat', 'stuffed him', 'dragged', and 'booted'. This vividly describes what happens in each case so that the reader can share the horror of the situation.
- **Repetition** is used throughout the poem to stress the issues, e.g. 'no query, no warning, no probe' and 'what business of mine… so long they don't take the yam'. Repetition of 'they' shows that the arrival of 'them' is a regular occurrence. The chant repeated at the end of each stanza becomes a mantra that people use to shield themselves from the real horror of the situation.
- **Similes**, e.g. 'soft like clay,' this portrays how severely the man was beaten.
- The last line of the poem describes the threat. The **alliteration** makes the line sound quiet and ominous, just like the jeep waiting on the lawn.
- **Metaphor:** 'froze my hungry hand'. This emphasises the terror the character feels by the fact that he can't eat, despite being very hungry.
- **Interrogatives:** 'What business… savouring mouth?' This question is repeated throughout the poem after every injustice, as though the character wants to justify his ignorance. He tries to get the reader to relate to his situation.
- The fact that the poem mentions 'one morning', 'one night', 'one day' and 'one evening', emphasises that injustice can occur at any time and will reoccur unless something is done to stop it.

Presents from My Aunts... Moniza Alvi

Content

The poem depicts the dilemmas faced by people of dual nationality; the young girl in the poem lives in England but was born in Pakistan.

The girl's aunts send her traditional clothes from Pakistan, but she states that she would rather be dressed in western fashions, feeling that the Pakistani clothes are too beautiful for her to wear. She mentions all the things of Pakistani origin: a salwar kameez and slippers, a camel-skin lamp, and some beautiful Indian jewellery for her mother (which was later stolen) and juxtaposes them with her life in England.

She remembers her journey from Pakistan by boat; this was a physical journey which becomes a cultural one in later life. She tries to remember her homeland by looking at old photos, and refers to the fact that there is now a territorial war in Kashmir.

Finally, she imagines herself back in Pakistan, looking through the gates of the Shalimar gardens. She is on the outside looking in which symbolises how she feels about living in England – that she is not fully integrated and that she belongs to two different cultures, which causes her internal conflict.

Setting

The poem is set in England. Images of Pakistan are given through her memories and the things she remembers from the old photos. In the last stanza, the girl imagines she is at the Shalimar ornamental gardens in Lahore, a city in Pakistan.

Themes

- The problems and frustration caused by belonging to two cultures.
- Fond memories of the past and childhood.
- How our cultural backgrounds shape who we will become.
- Alienation.

Style

- The poem starts with a reference to 'they,' an **impersonal address** which makes the girl seem detached from her aunts.
- The poem is written as a **first person narrative** to enable us to share her story and her emotions and to empathise with her.

- The first stanza contains **adjectives** to describe strong, rich colours (e.g. 'orange', 'gold', 'candy-striped') which represent the Asian culture.
- **Imagery** is used throughout the poem to enable us to visualise scenes and items, e.g. the salwar kameez is described as, 'glistening like an orange split open'. The lamp in line 27 is described as having colours 'like stained glass'.
- The poet mentions the 'fractured land / throbbing through newsprint'. Here she is referring to the conflict in Kashmir (an area belonging to both Pakistan and India). In amongst her personal reflections is a **political comment**.
- The conflict between her two cultures is depicted as the two are **juxtaposed** throughout the poem to reinforce the contrast between them.
- **Metaphors**, e.g. 'I was aflame', 'throbbing through newsprint' express the character's feelings.
- **Positive and negative diction** is juxtaposed throughout to contrast the two cultures and to show the problems that arise when the two cultures meet.

Hurricane Hits England Grace Nichols

Content

The hurricane makes the writer reminisce about her homeland of Guyana in the Caribbean. The hurricane is frightening but, ironically, it is also welcomed as it reminds her of her life in Guyana before she came to England.

The hurricane represents her inner turmoil at belonging to two cultures and so becomes a sympathetic background representing her turmoil as it awakens experiences and memories from her past. She refers to ancient gods and uses language from her Caribbean culture to show this turmoil. Finally, the character realises that, despite all the turmoil inside and all around her, all that matters is being alive and having a place on this Earth. This is the 'sweet mystery' of life. In many ways the poems reminds us of *This Room*.

Setting

The poem is set in England and Guyana in the present and the past, respectively.

Themes

- The force of nature.
- The strength of memories from the past and the effect they can have on shaping our experiences and the person that we will become.
- The importance of culture and language.
- The inner turmoil that people belonging to two different cultures experience: the outside storm reflects her inner battles.
- The value of life, despite its conflicts and turmoil.

Style

- **Negative diction**, e.g. 'howling', 'rage', 'dark' and 'fearful'. These words describe the storm on one level and the experience of living in a new land on another level.
- Traditional Caribbean gods are called upon – 'Huracan', 'Oya' and 'Shango' (gods of winds and storms). The woman's thoughts go back to her original place of birth and this is shown by using language from this culture.
- **Religious chants** are evoked in the last two stanzas: 'I am…', 'Come to…'. This shows the woman's respect for the storm (the power of nature) and the feelings that it creates in her.
- **Interrogatives:** there are many questions in the poem which show that the woman is questioning herself and her feelings, for example 'O why is my heart unchained?'. Here she is asking herself why she feels the way that she does (that is, tossed and uprooted by the storm).
- **Juxtaposition** of 'fearful' and 'reassuring' emphasises the woman's mixed feelings.
- **Pathetic fallacy:** the hurricane represents the woman's inner turmoil.
- The poem uses the **third person** ('she') in the first stanza, which shows that she doesn't feel comfortable with herself and how she fits in. It then changes to the **first person** ('I', 'me') which shows the woman is no longer scared; she accepts her situation and the reality that she finds herself in.

Comparing Poems

In order to obtain the top grades in the exam you will be expected to…
- compare the poems with insight, using relevant contextual details and close textual analysis
- analyse the writers' techniques and explore and empathise with the writers' ideas and attitudes
- show consistent insight and convincing / imaginative interpretations. (Make sure you have your own original thoughts and ideas.)
- produce structured and coherent responses.

In the exam you will be asked to compare poems. This may mean comparing the themes or setting through language (style) features, and / or layout and presentation. For example…
- Racial prejudice (theme) is discussed in *Nothing's Changed* and *Half-Caste*.
- Both *Blessing* and *Night of the Scorpion* are set in small, close-knit Indian villages (setting).
- The use of dialectal words and phrases (style) appear in both *Unrelated Incidents* and *Half-Caste*.
- *Blessing* and *This Room* look similar on the page (layout), set out in free verse.

Examiner's Tip

Look at identity, description, politics, and people; these are areas around which the questions could focus.

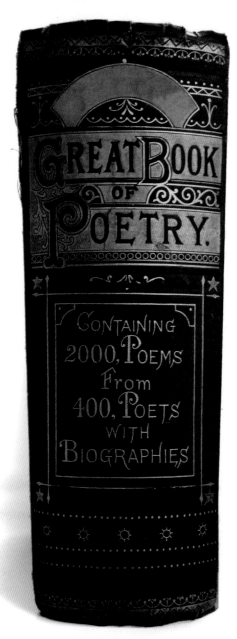

Writing Your Answer

The following example question will give you an idea of what you could be asked to do and how to develop your answer to gain a top grade.

Q. How do the writers in *Love After Love* and one other poem use language to portray inner conflict?

1. Look for key words in the question. Address each of the key words (and each bullet point, if you are given bullet points).
2. Think about the question you have been asked and choose your poem(s) carefully to allow you to answer the question well. Do not be afraid to use the more difficult poems; it is here that you can be more innovative and original in your comments.
3. Include a short introduction which is relevant and tightly focused on the question, mentioning which two poems you have chosen.
4. Look for similarities and differences in content, setting, themes, style, and presentation.
5. Use the PEE technique. Make your own personal observations but make sure you back them up with quotes and contextual evidence from the poems.
6. Make cross-references between your chosen poems – make apt and careful comparisons within and between the poems.
7. Conclude your answer by giving your overall opinion with reference to the question asked.

Exam Preparation

Practise comparing different poems. Pick out different pairs of poems and write down the similarities and differences you can see between them.

Comparing Poems

Common Themes

The following points describe some common themes in the poems. (They are listed only for revision purposes, not because they are the only ones you can compare.)

- **Origins and cultural identities (where you come from)** – *Limbo, Nothing's Changed, Island Man, Search for My Tongue, Unrelated Incidents, This Room, Presents from My Aunts in Pakistan,* and *Hurricane Hits England.*
- **The difficulty of belonging to two different cultures** – *Island Man, Search for My Tongue, Presents from My Aunts in Pakistan,* and *Hurricane Hits England.*
- **Anger at discrimination and racial prejudice in society** – *Nothing's Changed, Two Scavengers in a Truck, Two Beautiful People in a Mercedes, Unrelated Incidents, Half-Caste,* and *Not My Business.*
- **Alienation (being left out and feeling alone)** – *Nothing's Changed, Search for My Tongue, Presents from My Aunts in Pakistan,* and *Hurricane Hits England.*
- **The strength of childhood memories** – *Nothing's Changed, Night of the Scorpion, Presents from My Aunts in Pakistan,* and *Hurricane Hits England.*
- **Respect for ancient traditions / cultures / language** – *Limbo, Night of the Scorpion, Unrelated Incidents, Search for My Tongue, Presents from My Aunts in Pakistan,* and *Hurricane Hits England.*
- **Survival in spite of circumstances** – *Limbo, Blessing, Night of the Scorpion, Love After Love,* and *This Room.*
- **Acceptance of who you are** – *Love After Love, This Room, Presents from My Aunts in Pakistan,* and *Hurricane Hits England.*
- **Describing places in detail** – *Blessing, Night of the Scorpion, This Room,* and *Presents from My Aunts in Pakistan.*

- **Basic lifestyles and close communities** – *Blessing, Night of the Scorpion,* and *What Were They Like?*
- **Inner conflicts and political turmoil** – *What Were They Like?, Not my Business, Love After Love, This Room,* and *Hurricane Hits England.*
- **Expressing emotions through the language that is used (style)** – many of the poems use language in a particular way to portray certain emotions.

Exam Practice

Answer the following questions using the information above to help you choose which poems to discuss.

Q. Choose two poems that describe how difficult it is to belong to two different cultures. Compare the ways language is used in the poems to portray this.

Q. Choose two poems in which the poets' use of language shows anger at discrimination and racial prejudice in society. Compare how language is used in the poems to convey this.

When you have written some practice answers, use this checklist to see if they would achieve the top grades. Have you…

- thought of alternative interpretations and given your own thoughts and ideas?
- made cross-references between poems and compared them effectively whilst answering the question?
- compared the poems with insight, using relevant contextual details and close textual analysis (PEE)?
- analysed the techniques used to explore and empathise with the writers' ideas and attitudes?
- shown consistent insight and convincing / imaginative interpretation?
- produced structured and coherent responses?

Exam Tips and Exam Practice

Interpreting the Question

The following words and phrases often appear in the exam questions. Make sure you understand what they mean.

'The ideas'   Refers to the poem's themes.

'An event'   Refers to something that happens in the poem(s).

'Compare...'   Write about more than one poem – do not focus on just one.

'Contrast...'   Write about noticeable differences between two or more poems.

'Your response...'   What do you think the poem is about? Comment on what you have learned about the content, setting, themes and style.

'Your reaction...'   How does the poem make you feel when you read it? Comment on the themes and style of the poem.

'The methods used...'   Write about the words and stylistic features used.

'Ways things are described...'   Write about the words and stylistic features used to describe something or someone.

'What the poems are about'   Write about the content and themes of the poems.

Before the exam, make sure that you...

- know the poems well. Read each one through at least six times and make sure you know the meanings of any unfamiliar words
- learn the key points covered in this section of the guide
- are able to write confidently about content, setting, themes and style.

In the exam, make sure that you...

- read the questions carefully: take note of small words such as 'and' and 'or' (e.g. 'Compare the ways language *and* layout are used...')
- choose a question that you fully understand and are confident about answering well
- underline the key words in the question to help you focus on answering it successfully
- are aware of the time: you only have 45 minutes to write your answer.

Exam Practice

Answer each of the questions below in 45 minutes and ask your teacher to mark them. Remember to highlight the key words and use the PEE technique.

Q. Compare the ways in which the poets look at the difficulties in belonging to two cultures in *Presents from My Aunts in Pakistan* and one other poem.

Q. Compare the ways in which the poets use words to comment on society in *Unrelated Incidents* and one other poem.

Developing Your Answer

In the exam you will have to write about two poems. You should write about them simultaneously. Below is an example answer to the following question:

Q. Write about the ways in which *Blessing* and *Night of the Scorpion* use language to effectively portray the simplicity of village life and the impact it had on the poets' lives.

Exam Practice

Practice using the PEE technique: you will need to use it in the exam. Look at *Blessing* and *Night of the Scorpion* in your anthology and, for each of the nine points made in the example answer below, choose a quote that illustrates the point, then explain how it does so.

Introduction: clearly state what you are going to do. Refer back to the question and identify the poems you will discuss.

Give a brief summary of the content of each poem.

Use the PEE technique to make a point. These examples give a few of the points you could make about the use of language in these poems.

You *must* use a quote from the poem to provide evidence for every point you make and explain how the quote supports the point you are making.

The language employed in the poems 'Night of the Scorpion' and 'Blessing' effectively portrays the simplicity of village life. The writers' use of language shows how they value the communities which they are familiar with from their childhood, and how their experiences have been instrumental in making them who they are today.

The simplicity of village life is described in detail by both poets, but these simple scenes are depicted using vivid images and positive diction in both poems. 'Blessing' is written in the third person, as an observational piece, whilst 'Scorpion' is written in the first person making it seem more personal and involved.

'Blessing' describes what occurs in a small Indian village when a water pipe bursts and water cascades onto the streets. Water is such a rare commodity that it causes great excitement, especially amongst the children. The simplicity of life is seen as the people rush on to the streets carrying whatever containers they can find to collect this precious commodity. In 'Scorpion', the poet vividly describes what happens on the night that his mother is bitten by a scorpion. Both settings are described with almost pictorial quality. The reader can almost see a snapshot of the villages in their minds. Imagery and attention to detail make both poems effective in their portrayal of the scenes described.

'Blessing' starts by describing the dryness of the land using imagery and a simile **[add evidence and explanation]**... This effective use of language enables the reader to visualise the dryness of the land. This is compounded when the poet appeals to our senses by making us imagine the sounds of the water hitting the ground. Onomatopoeia is used **[add evidence and explanation]**... The water is referred to as a 'kindly god,' which shows us how much water is revered by the people in the community.

Religious diction can also be found in 'Scorpion' where it is used to evoke the chants of the villagers on the night that the boy's mother is stung. It stresses the simplicity of the people's lives that they believe such chants can cure the scorpion sting. In 'Scorpion' religious diction is used to show that all cultures rely on some higher being when disaster strikes. In 'Blessing', by contrast, religious diction is used to show the importance of the water **[add evidence and explanation]**...

The poet describes the water scene in 'Blessing' in such detail that we can picture it, just as we can with the night-time scene in the village in 'Scorpion'. This suggests that both poets believe that childhood memories, or memories from places in which we grow up, leave a long-lasting impression on our lives.

The simplicity of village life can be seen in the excitement of the children in 'Blessing' **[add evidence and explanation]**... Similarly, in 'Scorpion' the excitement of the villagers as they try to help the boy's mother is described through the effective use of imagery **[add evidence and explanation]**...

Use the correct language terms to make your points

Look at the differences as well as the similarities

Draw comparisons between the poems

Give your own opinions

Examiner's Tip

Spend 10–15 minutes considering the question, reading the poems, highlighting the parts of the poems you will refer to / quote, and planning your answer.

Exam Preparation

Highlight and label (with the criteria) all the places where the example response below fulfils the criteria to be awarded an A / A*. Can you write a better answer to the same question?

Both poets use imagery to help the reader to visualise the scene and both appeal to the senses in heightening this image.

However, in 'Blessing', following the beautiful description of the children, the poet contrasts this positive diction with the description of their bones as 'small' which shows that the children are undernourished due to the lack of water. The writer has remembered vividly the scene in the street but this is not all: it has left him with a long-lasting impression of how small and undernourished the children were in this village where water was such a rare commodity.

In 'Scorpion' the boy remembers the night his mother was bitten by a scorpion. It was a very wet night, which contrasts with the opening of 'Blessing'. As in 'Blessing', there is a close-knit community in 'Scorpion' **[add evidence and explanation]**...

In 'Scorpion', the poet builds up a picture of a close-knit community that is primitive in material terms but advanced in others – in the compassion the people show towards each other **[add evidence and explanation]**...

The repetition of the word 'more' towards the end of 'Scorpion' helps to convey the scene with the lights, the noise and the endless rain. The simplicity of the villagers' lives is meticulously described, from the descriptions of the mud huts to the arrival of the holy man.

The boy recalls how his father, who did not really believe in all the chants and curses, turned to strange remedies in an effort to aid his wife's recovery **[add evidence and explanation]**... After twenty four hours his mother recovered.

In a similar way to the way in which the water transforms a scene by its rapid arrival in 'Blessing', the drama in 'Scorpion' ends in a relatively short time. Perhaps both poets are stressing how a brief and dramatic event can have a real impact on the lives of the people it affects. In 'Scorpion', the mother's selflessness is obviously something that had a lasting impression on the poet **[add evidence and explanation]**...

To conclude, both poems seem, superficially, to portray scenes in basic villages which represent the simplicity of village life. However, they both end with a wider social or political comment. It is apparent that both poets admire and respect the villages and their inhabitants that they described; this can be seen by the reverential tone that runs through both poems. However, they also use their depictions to make wider social comments. 'Blessing' refers to the 'small' children, showing how undernourished they are and 'Night of the Scorpion' shows what a kind and thoughtful woman the poet's mother was; she would have preferred to die than have her children suffer.

2

Use the correct language terms to make your points

Look at the differences as well as the similarities

Draw comparisons between the poems

Give your own opinions

Conclusion: summarise the key points you have made in the main paragraphs (e.g. the language methods used) and relate them to both of the poems.

Writing to Inform, Explain or Describe

The Exam Question

Section B of Paper 2 will test you on your writing skills. It will contain three or four questions, of which you have to answer **one**. It is recommended that you spend 45 minutes on this question: five minutes for planning, 35 for the actual writing and five for checking. The questions cover three types of writing:

- writing to inform
- writing to explain
- writing to describe.

Although these types of writing are closely related, there are differences between them, which are discussed on the facing page. Usually, there is one question for each of the three purposes. There may also be a fourth question combining two of the three types of writing (e.g. inform and explain).

What is the examiner looking for?

The examiner wants to know how well you can write in English. Therefore, many of the marking criteria are the same as for Section B of Paper 1 (writing to argue, persuade or advise – see page 28), but the differences are in the purpose of the writing. To gain a grade A or A*, you must be able to demonstrate that you can do the following.

- Keep the reader interested in what you say and how you say it by communicating effectively in writing and using a variety of language techniques.
- Use an extensive vocabulary 'for effect': do not always choose the most simple and obvious words, but think carefully about meaning and connotation.
- Vary sentence structures, possibly using repetition, contrast, parallel phrases and clauses.
- Use a range of punctuation accurately. A 'range' includes full stops, commas, question marks, apostrophes, inverted commas, exclamation marks (but use these sparingly!), dashes, colons and semi-colons (see page 4).
- Write in clear paragraphs, ordered so that the whole piece makes sense and can be easily followed, but not necessarily in the most obvious way.
- Write well in Standard English.
- Develop and show a strong personal style.
- Spell words correctly.
- Write clearly for the specified purpose and audience.
- Write in an original and sophisticated manner in different forms.
- Use techniques such as humour, irony and satire when appropriate in the context.
- Write neatly and organise your work clearly.

At this level, your work should be a pleasure to read.

This section of the revision guide will look at writing to inform and writing to explain together, as they have many similarities (see pages 74–85). Writing to describe is quite different and will be covered separately (see pages 86–93).

Wadefield High School

Dear Parent / Guardian,

I am writing to inform you about some important events in the coming term. Year 11 pupils will commence study leave on 20 May. Half term will be from Monday 29 May until Friday 2 June. Monday 5 June will be an INSET day for the staff, so pupils will not be returning until Tuesday 6 June.

Wadefield High School, 115 Broad Street, Upperthong, Wadefield WD1 1TT
t: 01924 683377   f: 01924 683378   e: wadefieldhighschool@co.uk

Writing to Inform

METALS

Metals are good conductors. Conduction occurs in metals because as the metal becomes hotter its vibrating ions gain more kinetic energy.

Science   27

Writing to Explain

Lake Garda

Lake Garda, Italy's largest, is a dazzling expanse of blue originally created by ice-age glaciation. The glorious surrounding scenery varies dramatically from the severe grandeur of its snow-capped mountains to the tranquil serenity of its sandy shores and seductive vine-covered hills.

Writing to Describe

Writing to Inform

Informing involves telling people the facts about a subject. A successful piece of informative writing leaves its audience knowing more about its subject than they did before. To achieve this, you must…

- present a wide range of interesting information, focused on the question
- communicate facts in a way that will keep your readers interested and make them think
- write from a non-biased point of view.

A simple example of writing to inform is the letter above, from a head teacher to parents, informing them about forthcoming events in school. It informs the audience what will happen; the writer does not have to argue a case or persuade the audience about anything. It may go on, however, to *explain* things in more detail.

Writing to Explain

An explanation goes further than simply giving information, telling the audience more about the subject of the writing, perhaps saying how something works or why something is as it is. You must…

- present the readers with interesting facts
- provide cogent, detailed explanations of the facts in an original way
- write from a non-biased point of view.

A simple example of writing to explain is the extract from a science book, above. This extract explains why and how conduction occurs in metals (it firstly *informs* the reader that conduction can occur in metals).

Writing to Describe

Descriptive writing involves portraying something / someone / somewhere to your audience. Descriptive writing still informs, but can give more scope for the imaginative use of language, often giving opportunities for developing a personal viewpoint. You should…

- provide a range of interesting, detailed descriptions
- use a range of descriptive language techniques, such as metaphors, similes and onomatopoeia, to help the audience create a picture in their minds
- draw the readers into the world you are describing.

A simple example of writing to describe is the extract above, from a travel book. It gives information and explains why the lake looks like it does, but its chief purpose is to paint a picture through the effective use of descriptive language.

You can see how closely the three types of writing are linked. Whichever question you answer, your writing will include elements of informing, explaining and describing. The difference is one of emphasis. You must consider the purpose of your writing and how this affects the way you write.

Purpose, Audience, Form and Language

This part of the book will focus on writing to inform and writing to explain.

Remember, the first things you need to know when starting to write are…
– **what is the purpose of the writing?**
– **who is your audience?**

Purpose

We know that the purpose of the writing in this section of the exam is to inform, explain or describe (see pages 86–93 for writing to describe). Here are some examples of the type of questions you could be asked on informing and explaining in this section of the exam.

Q. Write a letter to your Member of Parliament **informing** him / her about what it is like to be a young person living in your area.

Q. If you could meet anyone who had ever lived, who would it be? **Explain** the reasons for your choice.

Q. Write **informatively** about your favourite leisure pursuit and **explain** why you do it.

The purpose of each question is obvious as the key word is printed in bold. You have no excuse for misunderstanding the question.

The first question could be about an experience you might have had, but it is expressed in quite an impersonal way, so beware of talking only about yourself. A top candidate would be required to present a range of information from various sources; this could mean using the experiences (real or imagined) of your friends, as well as accounts of events reported in newspapers and perhaps even government statistics. Of course, you will not have such things with you in the exam but, for the purpose of the exam, it is acceptable to make them up. To write

effectively about these experiences you might need to explain why or how things happen, and give your own feelings and opinions. However, the emphasis is on informing so you need to be able to write about them in a fairly detached, unbiased manner.

The second question asks you to explain and justify your feelings and opinions. You still need to give information, as your audience will need to know something about the person, but this time the focus is on explaining. The purpose of your writing is to help readers to understand why you want to meet your chosen subject. You could get a question which asks you to explain something less personal, like how to use the Internet, but such questions are not common.

The third question asks for both information and explanation. You should try to focus equally on both. Your reader needs to know all about your hobby in order to understand your reasons for doing it.

Exam Preparation

Read this question, which asks for both information and explanation, and think about how it differs from the three questions discussed.

Q. Choose something you feel strongly about. Write **informatively** about it and **explain** why you feel as you do.

Examiner's Tips

If the purpose of the writing is to inform, focus on who, what, when and where.

If the purpose of the writing is to explain, focus on how and why.

join the family

We were wondering if you'd like to join the innocent family. Don't worry – it's not some weird cult. It's just our way of staying in touch with the people who drink our drinks i.e. you. Every week we'll email you our news and give you the chance to win lots of drinks. We'll also invite you to nice events like Fruitstock (our free festival) and maybe even send you the odd present if you're lucky.

If you fancy joining, visit www.innocentdrinks.co.uk/family

Audience

When you consider how to write for your audience, ask yourself…

- do I know the person / people I am writing to / for?
- how old are they?
- what do I have in common with them?
- what response am I trying to get from them?

Form

You may be asked to write in a specific form. This could be a letter, a leaflet, an article etc. (See pages 80–82.)

Language

The language you write in must be appropriate for the audience; you need to use the correct register (tone). 'Register' refers to the style of language used in a specific situation. It includes the 'tone of voice' and the level of formality employed, and is determined by both subject matter and audience. The answers to the questions above should help you decide on the register of your writing. Is it formal and businesslike or informal and chatty? What kind of vocabulary will you use? Will you use technical or specialised language, or more everyday language that most people can understand?

Informal Language and Register

When writing for fellow students or other people of your own age, your register will probably be informal. You might not know them personally, but you have a lot in common with them and this will influence your language. You might…

- address them directly, using the second person ('you'), and the first person ('I' or 'we') to show that you identify with them and their concerns
- use abbreviations and contractions such as 'you've'
- use the kind of vocabulary you use when talking to your friends, but don't overdo it and do not use 'text language' unless asked to do so (very unlikely!)
- use alliteration, similes, metaphors or even rhyme to achieve a lively tone
- make references that teenagers will understand but adults might not, for example to 'cult' television shows, popular celebrities, films and music.

Formal Language and Register

An older audience, like your teachers, probably wouldn't appreciate an informal tone and might not take you seriously. For a formal tone, you should…

- use the second person, but not as often or in such a familiar way as in informal writing, e.g. 'you might be interested to know…', rather than 'did you know that…?'
- use full words, not contractions
- avoid slang – these people are not your friends
- use a range of punctuation, including colons and semi-colons, but avoid exclamation marks
- use complex sentences and correctly employ a range of connectives (see page 35)
- use the passive voice to create a less personal tone
- be polite, using phrases such as 'I should be grateful if you would…'
- consider using specialised language, perhaps referring to things that are important to your audience, for example, writing to teachers you might mention the national curriculum or school league tables.

Planning Your Answer

There are many ways to plan and by now you have probably established a way that suits you.

When writing to inform or explain, a good way to decide what to include in your answer is to try answering these six basic questions about your subject:

1. What?
2. Who?
3. Where?
4. When?
5. How?
6. Why?

You might produce the plan (below) in response to the following question.

Q: Write **informatively** about your favourite leisure pursuit and **explain** why you do it.

- What?   Dancing – Ballroom (Fox Trot, Waltz, Tango etc.); Latin (Rumba, Cha-cha, Salsa)
- Who?   Me, my dance teacher, students, professionals
- Where? Opal Dance School – local / national competitions – ballrooms – places dances come from
- When?   Me: every Saturday, Wednesday, last 8 years. The dances: origins / history
- How?   Basics of dances, rehearsal, steps, music, costumes
- Why?   Enjoyment, exercise, competition, excitement

This plan shows that there is plenty of material on which to base a good answer. The next step is to organise the answer. Your audience should not be aware that you are answering these questions and the 'hows' and 'whys' should arise naturally out of the 'whats' and 'whos', forming a seamless and subtle whole. You need a striking (and perhaps unusual or intriguing) opening that makes the reader want to read on, and a strong ending that may 'tie up loose ends' or leave the reader wondering.

The second plan (below) is a paragraph plan for the same piece of writing.

---

1. Opening – the excitement of my big competition / anticipation – what is it?
2. How and why I got involved – first impressions
3. Popularity of different dances / what they are about
4. Latin dancing and Ballroom dancing – the differences
5. My favourite dance – what it involves and why I like it
6. Costumes / music – the glamour and the sequins
7. Competitions – my love / hate relationship with them (and with my competitors!)
8. Back to that competition – what happened?

This plan covers all the questions, giving both information and explanation, and shows that the writer has plenty to say on the subject.

What should you write about?

'Write about what you know.' This is the advice that is often given to writers. However, do not be afraid to use your imagination – writing about what you know does not necessarily mean sticking to the facts.

Some questions do not seem to offer a lot of choice. For example, if you are asked to write an article giving information about GCSE options at your school, you can only write about the options that exist. But if you are asked to give a report on an event, there are many possible events you could choose from – national events, school events, family events etc. Remember that A / A* candidates are the ones who take risks and do things that would not occur to others.

If you are asked to write about something like an event, you might choose one that you found interesting, exciting, funny or even extremely embarrassing. You wouldn't normally choose to write about something that you found boring; if you do, your writing will have to be exceptionally witty to entertain your audience. An A* candidate might well be able to do that.

If you are asked about more personal subjects, such as your hobbies, choose something that you enjoy doing – preferably something unusual that other candidates are unlikely to write about. Ensure you have the knowledge to explain your subject in a detailed and interesting way, so that your enthusiasm comes through in your writing.

Examiner's Tip

Always write in paragraphs and ensure that the paragraphs are connected in a variety of ways. An A / A* student should create a coherent structure with paragraphs that are fluently linked.

Exam Preparation

Create a plan, using the six basic questions, for the question above. (Have you got enough material for a two to three page essay?)

To gain a top grade you need to use a variety of sentence structures appropriate to your purpose and audience.

A **simple sentence**, e.g. 'the cat (subject) sat (verb) on the mat (object)' can be very effective, for example, in giving emphasis to an important point. However, if you use only simple sentences you will not gain high marks for your writing.

A **compound sentence**, e.g. 'the cat sat on the mat and drank the milk' can be used effectively (although this example is not very sophisticated). Both simple and compound sentences can be especially useful in writing to inform, explain or describe when you are trying to convey simplicity or finality, for example…

- The Sun is a light source but the moon is not. **Inform**
- It was closed so we went home. **Explain**
- She shrieked piercingly and ran off. **Describe**

A **complex sentence** consists of the basic structure – 'noun; main verb; object' – but the main clause is qualified by **subordinate clauses**, which can come before, within or after the main clause, for example…

- <u>Sitting on the mat</u>, the cat drank the milk.
- The cat, <u>which was sitting on the mat</u>, drank the milk.

You can have any number of subordinate clauses in a complex sentence as long as you have a main verb and the sentence makes sense. This means complex sentences are useful in descriptive writing, for example…

- <u>Having returned late from a midnight hunt</u>, the cat, <u>who was famished and was now the object of everybody's attention – oh, how they adored that cat –</u> slowly drank the milk.

You may think the example above is a bit too complex. When judging whether your sentences are too long and complicated, think about whether your audience might lose track of the point you are trying to make.

A **fragment** is not really a sentence at all, but is punctuated like one. It may lack a subject, object or verb, for example…

- The cat!
  This fragment has no verb and no object.
- Drinking milk.
  This fragment has no subject or auxiliary verb.

Fragments should be used sparingly, for dramatic effect. They can be effective in descriptive writing as long as it is clear from their context that their use is deliberate and not the result of poor punctuation.

Examiner's Tip

A series of very short, simple sentences can help to convey excitement and speed. However, writing that consists entirely of simple and compound sentences lacks variety and is incapable of conveying mature and sophisticated ideas.

Exam Preparation

This passage contains only simple sentences. Rewrite it so that it contains one simple sentence, one compound sentence, at least one complex sentence and one fragment:

The dog barked. I went outside. I couldn't see him. The moonlight shone on the grass. The trees looked sinister. I was worried about the dog. What had he found? I went to look for him. There were bushes around me. I was scared. Everything was silent. I heard a scream.

Structure: Sentences

Active and Passive Voices

You should demonstrate that you can use both the active and passive voices. Again, this adds variety to your writing. The **active** voice is best for writing about action: it gives a sense of immediacy as well as putting the emphasis on the person who does the action (the subject), for example...
– The dog bit the boy.
– The governors have appointed a new head teacher.
– Foxes hunt and kill rabbits.

The **passive** voice changes the emphasis, so that the object is in the place of the subject, for example...
– The boy was bitten by the dog.
– A new head teacher has been appointed by the governors.
– Rabbits are hunted and killed by foxes.

In all three of the passive sentences above, the object of the action (the subject of the action in the active sentences) can be taken out and the sentence still makes sense.

High-achieving candidates are expected to demonstrate that they can use the passive voice effectively. It is especially useful in impersonal writing (see page 83).

Imperatives

Imperatives can be useful in writing to inform or explain. For example, when explaining how to make a cake, you might use a phrase such as 'mix together the flour and butter'. If you are asked to inform someone about a forthcoming event you might address the reader directly with a phrase such as 'be there by eight o'clock'.

Parallel Phrasing

Parallel phrasing is much-loved by English examiners. As with many other aspects of sentence structure, it is quite possible that you are already using it. It means using (in a pair or sequence) two or more phrases that are constructed in the same way, for example...
– The pavements shone with virgin snow; the windows glittered with morning frost; and my heart filled with new-born hope.
– She was neither excited by the prospect of fame, nor depressed by the expectation of failure.

Tenses

In English, there are three basic tenses: past, present and future. However, there are different ways of forming each of these tenses.

Past Tense
• Simple past: I watched, I wrote
• Past continuous: I was watching, I was writing
• Perfect: I have watched, I have written
• Pluperfect: I had watched, I had written

Present Tense
• Simple present: I watch, I write
• Present continuous: I am watching, I am writing

In English, the **future tense** can be formed in a number of ways, for example, I will watch, I am going to write, I will be watching etc.

Language: Humour and Irony

In the past, examiners have commented that effective use of humour and irony is a notable feature of the work of the best candidates. Humour and irony can be used effectively in all types of writing, as long as it is used appropriately.

The problem with trying to introduce humour into your writing is that if you try too hard it will not work. Humour should arise naturally from the content of your writing and be the result of your personal view of the world. For example, a description of a place or person can be humorous, whether through a grotesque caricature, or through a gentle yet stinging irony. However, if you feel inspired to write a serious piece, without a trace of humour, do so. Humour is not compulsory.

Irony

Irony involves a discrepancy between what is said and what is meant. The reader needs to understand that the writer is being ironic, so clues must be provided by the context. Irony is sometimes referred to as **sarcasm** (but that term usually refers to speech when it can be detected through tone of voice). In writing, it will be more subtle. There are three main forms of irony:

1. **Antiphrasis**, the simplest and shortest form, is when words are used to mean the opposite of their usual meaning, for example…
   - Having been caught smoking again, I was sent to see **my dear friend** the headmistress.

2. **Litotes** is an ironic use of understatement, using the word 'not' to say something is its opposite, for example…
   - The school trip was, as always, punctuated by **not infrequent** bouts of vomiting.

3. **Meiosis** refers to something in terms which make it sound less important than it is, for example, if a bad wound was referred to as a scratch. It can also be used to insult, for example, referring to writing as 'scribbling'.

You could use **puns** and double meanings to demonstrate your skills. A lot of humour can be gained from the **juxtaposition** of two apparently unconnected ideas.

One of the most endearing and effective ways of employing humour is to use it against yourself, perhaps recounting an anecdote about a time when you made a complete fool of yourself.

Examiner's Tip

If you feel like being funny, be funny. Examiners plough through hundreds of answers, many of them very dull. Sometimes they appreciate a good laugh.

Form

Articles

This section of the exam often has a question which asks candidates to write an article. This may be an article for a newspaper, a magazine or a website. (See pages 37–38 for more on writing articles.) If you look at a range of articles for these three media, you will see that the style and tone depend on the subject and the intended audience as well as on their purpose.

Presentation

You do not want your answer to look like an article, but you do want it to read like one. Using the following features of newspaper and magazine articles can help.

A headline: this is the title of the article. It may be serious or funny and often uses language features like puns, alliteration or rhyme. For example…
– Winter Wonderland
Alliteration is used to grab the reader's attention, but it does not say in detail what the article is actually about.

A strapline: this comes just above or below the headline and introduces the story, explaining the headline. For example…
– Santa's grotto and delicious festive fare add a flavour of Christmas as part of the annual celebrations.

This explains what the article will be about and attracts readers by using alliteration and a metaphor to give a sense of excitement and enjoyment.

Sub-headings: these are used to organise and break up the text, making it easy to follow and allowing the reader to skip to the bits that interest him / her most.

Each sub-heading may introduce two or three paragraphs. Sub-headings can also help your planning: note down the most important things you want to write about and then put them in order. For example, planning for a football report might look something like this (the numbers give the order of the sub-headings):

Grudge match against Sutton	1	Hartson's header	3
Half-time honours even	4	Penalty joy	7
Sutton scores first	2	Smithy scores	5
Sutton captain sent off	6	Freshfields in final	8

These rough notes could make effective sub-headings, helping to create a lively and engaging article. This paragraph plan follows chronological order, which can be a little dull. Think about how else you could arrange it.

Examiner's Tip

Presentation is not important, as long as the examiner can read your writing. You will not get extra marks for trying to make your paper look like a real article with columns and pictures; you may even lose marks because it wastes time and distracts the examiner from the content of your writing.

Exam Preparation

Try planning an answer to the following question.

Q. Write an article for a school newspaper in which you **inform** other students about a forthcoming event either in school or in the local community.

Letters

Writing in the form of a letter might come up in this section of the exam. If it does, you must consider your audience and the appropriate tone. The identity of your audience determines the form of the letter.

Informal Letters

An informal letter might be a letter to a friend, a relative or someone you know very well. You would write your own address and the date in the top right hand corner, use the person's first name and end with an informal 'signing off'. Look at this example:

> 16 Acacia Cottages
> Little Puddington
> Lancashire
>
> 16th April 2006
>
> Dear Jill,
>
> It was great to hear from you! I'm really well, thanks. I'm still working for the school but I've now been promoted to Head of Year, and I'm really enjoying it.
>
> Tom and I bought a house together and will be moving in in a couple of months. You and James will have to come and stay. It'd be great to see you.
>
> I'll ring you soon and we'll arrange to meet up.
>
> See you soon,
>
> Love, Lizzie

Formal Letters

Recipients of formal letters would include teachers, employers, newspaper editors – anyone you do not know well. As well as your own address, you put the recipient's address on the left of the letter. You should address the recipient formally, and sign off your letter formally: 'Yours sincerely' if you have the person's name; 'Yours faithfully' if you do not. A person whose name you do not know is addressed as 'Sir' or 'Madam'. Look at this example:

> 16 Acacia Cottages
> Little Puddington
> Lancashire
>
> Mr M Parker
> Manager
> 10 High Street
> Greenton
> Lancashire
>
> 14th April 2006
>
> Dear Mr Parker
>
> I am writing to inform you of my change of address. As of the 24th May, my address will be as follows:
>
> 42 Pinecroft Avenue
> Lipton, Little Puddington
> Lancashire
> LN3 5UF
>
> Please amend my details to take account of this change of address. My telephone number will remain the same. If you need any further details, don't hesitate to contact me.
>
> Yours sincerely,
>
> *Elizabeth Orpington*
> Elizabeth Orpington

Exam Preparation

Here is part of a formal letter to the school governors informing them about the school's litter problem. Using the advice given so far, rewrite it to address fellow students.

> We students have become very concerned lately about the amount of litter to be found around the school. Almost every day, students arrive in their classrooms to find the floors are covered in sweet wrappers, empty crisp packets and discarded drink cans. The corridors are even worse. Very few bins are provided and they are all overflowing with litter...

Form

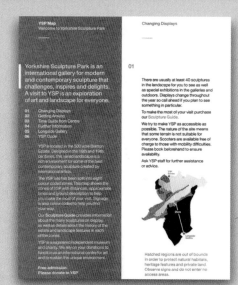
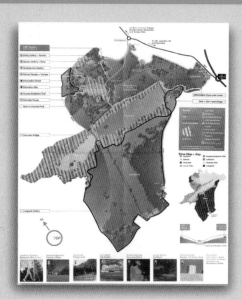

Leaflets

It is not often that a question comes up in this section of the exam which asks you to write a leaflet or information sheet – but it might happen. If you choose to answer such a question, don't waste time trying to make your paper look like a real leaflet, but think about using headlines, straplines and sub-headings.

Problems with Writing Leaflets

The biggest problem that candidates find with writing for leaflets is the fact that real leaflets tend to be written in simple language and often use presentation devices such as bullet points. It can be hard, therefore, to use the range of language techniques that achieves good marks. Also, if you are simply telling people facts, there is not much room for developing a distinctive style in your writing.

Use language to make your piece interesting and entertaining, perhaps including alliteration, rhyme, puns, metaphors and similes. Your challenge, as a potential top-grade student, is to write the text for a leaflet that is quirky and original, and shows off your language skills.

Exam Preparation

Study some leaflets and see what they are informing you about. Do they also contain explanation and / or description? Or are they giving advice or persuading you to do something (so being the kind of writing you are asked to do in Paper 1)? Look for examples of different language techniques.

Discursive Essays

In recent years more than half the questions in the writing to inform, explain or describe section have asked for 'discursive writing' or a traditional essay, rather than writing in a specific form such as an article or letter. Here are two examples of the type of questions which may come up in this section of the exam and do not require you to write in a specific form:

Q. Explain how you feel at the moment and why you feel this way.

Q. Think about something you made, of which you were proud. **Explain** how you made it and what your feelings were about it.

These two questions have two things in common; they both ask you to explain something, and they both ask you to write about personal matters.

One difference between discursive essay writing and writing in other forms is that you are less likely to use the second person ('you') in discursive essays. You might use it in the introduction to grab the reader's attention, or as part of a rhetorical question. However it should be used sparingly; you do not know who your audience is so it is difficult to address them directly.

Exam Practice

Try answering the following question in 45 minutes.

Q. Think about an occasion when you did something you now regret. **Explain** why you did it and why you regret it.

Personal and Impersonal Writing

Personal Writing

Whatever form of writing the question asks for, a good answer will include elements of both personal and impersonal writing.

The most personal type of writing is in a diary, where you enter your private thoughts, but do not intend them to be read by others. Autobiographies and letters to friends are other examples of personal writing.

Anecdotes

It is a good idea to use anecdotes in your writing to make it more personal. Anecdotes are very brief personal stories, often amusing, and used to illustrate a point. They are especially useful for introducing your subject. Look at this introduction to an essay on dancing, in response to the question about leisure pursuits.

> The biggest night of my life: my heart pounds like a drum. I check my make-up in the dressing room mirror – Madame calls it 'slap' and tonight it looks as if I've been slapped – I'm much too red. But it will have to do. What's next? The hair: well, there's plenty of it and it's in the right place. I must stop being so negative – remember what Madame said: 'Positive thinking, darling, positive thinking!'. I am positive. We will win. I'm calm and I'm positive. Until I notice my shoes…

This opening uses personal writing (the anecdote) to 'hook' the reader. Always remember, however, what the question is asking you to do – explain and inform. It demands that you tell the readers things they did not already know, not just about you, but about your hobby. To do this you also need to include an impersonal element.

In the essay plan on page 76 the tone switches from personal to impersonal in the third paragraph. This paragraph opens up the essay so it is no longer just about the writer but about dancing in general. Here you could make use of facts you have learned; you could discuss the history / origins of ballroom dancing, mention statistics, perhaps about the number of dance schools in the country or the number of people who go to classes, and even give information about physiology.

Impersonal Writing

Impersonal writing is when you are not writing about yourself. You may be writing about an event, a place, a country, a person (other than yourself or your friends and family), an activity etc. that has nothing to do with you.

Impersonal Writing Tips

- When the tone is impersonal there will be less use of the first person and more use of the third person.
- There may be impersonal constructions such as the passive voice (see page 78).
- Even though the writing is impersonal, your style can still be lively and you can include a personal viewpoint, as long as you are giving information and explanations.
- Show that you have a lot of information, drawn from various sources, and sound as if you know what you are talking about.

Exam Preparation

What do you know a lot about? Write an opening paragraph for a discursive essay in a personal tone that will invite the reader into your world.

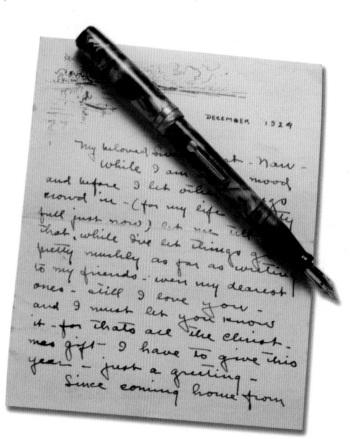

Writing to Inform or Explain

If you are writing to inform or explain, your purpose is to communicate information and facts to your audience, and explain them. Readers should know more about a subject after they have read a piece of informative writing. They should clearly understand a subject after they have read a piece of writing whose purpose is to explain. There is a variety of language techniques you can use when writing to inform or explain.

Techniques in Writing to Inform or Explain

Here is a summary of some of the techniques you could use to make your writing effective as an informative or explanatory piece.

- **Modal verbs** are useful in writing to explain as they create a polite tone.
- Suitable **connectives** to link the information and explanations.
- **Formal tone** to make your opinion seem more credible.
- **Rule of three:** group ideas in threes, building the impact.

- **Lists:** give a range of examples, perhaps using repetition or alliteration to link them.
- **Infinitives** can give a formal tone to a piece of writing. Many pieces of writing whose purposes are to inform or explain require a formal tone.
- **No omission / contraction:** if you use omission / contraction, it will give an informal tone to the writing so it is best to use full words, e.g. 'will not' instead of 'won't', 'could have' instead of 'could've'.
- **Passive voice:** this is very useful in writing to explain as it creates a polite tone which is not patronising.
- **Conditional sentences** are effective as they express cause and effect, therefore assisting an explanation.
- **Past tenses:** try to vary these between the simple tense (I climbed), the past continuous (I was climbing), the perfect (I have climbed) and the pluperfect (I had climbed).
- **Second person:** use the second person, but not as often or in such a familiar way in formal writing as in informal writing, e.g. 'you might be interested to know…', rather than 'did you know that…?'

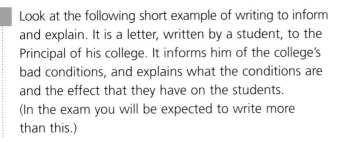

Look at the following short example of writing to inform and explain. It is a letter, written by a student, to the Principal of his college. It informs him of the college's bad conditions, and explains what the conditions are and the effect that they have on the students.
(In the exam you will be expected to write more than this.)

Exam Practice

Q. Write an article for a teenagers' magazine in which you **explain** the importance of a good education.

Q. Write a letter to your new pen-friend, **informing** him / her about your life and **explaining** to him / her why you do what you do.

Modal verbs

Suitable connectives

Rule of three
and lists

Infinitives

Passive voice

Conditional sentences

Second person

Appropriate use
of a range of
punctuation

Full words instead of
contractions

Fragments

Parallel phrasing

Dear Mr Fletcher,

I am writing, on behalf of the student council of Greenacres College, to inform you of our concerns about the environment. When I use the word 'environment', I refer not to the state of the planet, the plight of the world's wildlife or the future of the eco-system, but to the everyday environment in which we all work.

We students have become very concerned lately about the amount of litter to be found around the school. Almost every day, students arrive in their classrooms to find the floors are covered in all manner of detritus: sweet wrappers, empty crisp packets, and discarded drink cans. Desks are embellished daily with fresh graffiti (the details of which would make you blush) and their undersides studded with stale gum.

The corridors are even worse. Very few bins are provided and they are all overflowing with litter. Small, plastic, swing-top bins, designed for suburban kitchens, are clearly not adequate for the needs of a busy college like ours. Again, there is graffiti, with notice boards continually defaced. It is incredibly disappointing to see our beautifully presented, proudly displayed work violated by the crudest of obscenities. This will not motivate the students of Greenacres.

Finally, I turn to the foyer — the first and last impression received by any visitor. Not the warmest of welcomes. It is drab. It is uncared for. It is unfriendly. No stranger who enters that space could fail to be underwhelmed; no distinguished visitor could leave it without a sense of relief.

These are the facts which I place before you on behalf of my fellow students. I should be most grateful if you, as Principal of Greenacres College, would give them the consideration they deserve. We, the students, would be only too happy to present you with our own proposals for improvement. I look forward to receiving your response.

Yours sincerely,

Alex Burns

Purpose, Audience and Form

This part of the book will focus on writing to describe.

Purpose

The main difference between writing to inform or explain and writing to describe is that 'describe' questions give you more opportunity to be truly creative and original. They may present you with the best opportunity to show off your A/A* potential. As well as demonstrating that you have a wide vocabulary and can use a variety of sentence structures for effect, as required by the mark scheme, you can be adventurous with structure and form, showing off your unique style. But be warned: you must not write a story. There may be an element of narrative writing in your work but the focus must be on description, not plot.

Here are some examples of the kind of questions you might get.

Q. Describe your ideal holiday.

Q. Describe a place where you enjoy spending time.

Q. Think of a recent trip you have taken and **describe** how you got to your destination.

Q. Describe a park in the summer and **describe** it in the winter.

At first sight these questions may seem dull and undemanding. In reality, they present countless possibilities. It is up to you to make your work stand out from the bland and uninspiring mass. All four of these questions can be answered in different ways.

An 'ideal holiday' could be a holiday you have been on, one you have heard about, or the kind of holiday you would like to have in the future and can only dream about now.

A 'place where you enjoy spending your time' could be a real place like a leisure centre or your bedroom, or a fantasy world full of magical and exotic sights and sounds.

The question about journeys asks you to write about 'a trip you have taken', suggesting it must be a real experience. But if you feel that you have never been on a trip that would inspire a good answer, you can make one up, or adopt a persona and let your imagination run wild.

The fourth question asks for two descriptions of the same place. Similar questions could ask you to describe somewhere at night and in the morning, or in the past and the future. You could write two separate descriptions, one after the other, but it might be more impressive to weave together the descriptions of the two places or times from the start, comparing and contrasting as you go.

Exam Preparation

Take each of the first three questions on this page in turn and 'brainstorm' at least three different places/experiences that you could describe for each answer.

Example 1

26 Hill View
Norwich
Norfolk

Dear Claire,

That gloomy old house on the corner has changed beyond recognition. Where once it seemed to struggle for air in a dank oppressive jungle, now it rejoices in an artist's palette of flowers: sky-blue azaleas; blood-red poppies; snow-white lilies and a riot of variegated roses...

Example 2

26 Hill View
Norwich
Norfolk

Dear Tom,

The house next to ours is the corner house. Larger and more impressive than all the others in the street, it used to belong to the ancient Mrs Gorgonberry, and was an outward manifestation of her inner being. Dank ivy hung menacingly across the front door; a jungle of weeds denied entry to visitors; the house seemed to struggle for air. But now it has new owners...

Audience

Questions on writing to describe do not usually specify an audience but you might get a question like this:

Q. Write a letter to a pen friend who lives abroad, **describing** the area in which you live.

Just as with inform and explain questions, if the describe question specifies an audience, you should ask yourself questions about the intended audience:
- do I know the person / people I am writing to / for?
- how old are they?
- what do I have in common with them?
- what response am I trying to get from them?

Imagine you are asked to write a description of your neighbourhood for an old friend who has moved away. Remember, this is not an 'inform' question, so facts and figures are not necessary. You can assume a certain amount of prior knowledge on your friend's behalf; he / she would probably only be interested in changes to the neighbourhood. You need to use all your powers of description to make those changes 'live' for him / her.

Read example 1 (opposite). The references to what the house used to look like indicate that the writer and the reader share prior knowledge of it.

If, on the other hand, you were writing for a pen friend who had never visited you, you would need to explain a bit more. Read example 2 (opposite). In this version the writer provides background information to give the reader a more complete picture.

Form

You may be asked to write a description in a particular form, e.g. an article for a magazine or newspaper, or a letter like the examples on this page (see pages 80–82 for how to write in different forms). Usually, however, a describe question will not specify a particular form.

Exam Preparation

Try writing a paragraph about the house on the corner for an alien from another planet.

Planning Your Answer

Sometimes candidates have difficulty approaching a piece of descriptive writing. Some construct complex narratives, forgetting that the focus is on description. Others, when writing descriptions of real places, waste time explaining how they got there: for example, if they are writing about a place they have been to on holiday, they mention everything from getting up in the morning and boarding the plane to arriving home a week later.

You need to think about what you are being asked to describe and focus on that.

Big to Small Technique

An effective way of planning a piece of descriptive writing is to go from 'big to small'. Imagine you are a camera gradually closing in on an object. Start by describing your subject in general terms, as if seen from a distance. As you get closer and more involved, your description becomes more detailed, until you focus on something small but significant. Opposite is a 'big to small' plan for an answer based on the question about 'a place where you enjoy spending your time'. The candidate has chosen to write about his grandparents' house.

A piece of writing based on this plan would keep readers interested by bringing them gradually into the world being described. It is as if the reader is being brought to the house and shown round it.

My Grandparents' House

Paragraph 1:   Its location: far away from the city (contrast) → by the sea

Paragraph 2:   The approach: the lane → the front garden → looking at the house

Paragraph 3:   The layout: design → style and décor of the rooms

Paragraph 4:   The kitchen → old-fashioned; the living room → comfortable, reflecting their personalities and backgrounds

Paragraph 5:   The people in the house: grandmother welcoming me → memories and ghosts

Paragraph 6:   In my bedroom: at home yet not at home: my shelves → my books

Paragraph 7:   Something special (a book that's always there) and what it means to me

Paragraph 8:   How I feel when I wake up in the morning → what I see, hear, smell etc. Refer back to the beginning

Exam Preparation

Write a 'big to small' plan for a completely different interpretation of the question:
Q. Describe a place where you enjoy spending time.

Using the Senses

Another effective way to plan your descriptive piece is to use the five senses: sight, sound, smell, touch and taste. Opposite is an example of a plan, using the senses, based on the following question.

Q. Think of a recent trip you have taken and **describe** how you got to your destination.

The writer has chosen to describe a train journey through a foreign country on the way to visit a relative. The next step is to put her thoughts in order. This can be very straightforward if you arrange the essay chronologically, as a journey has a beginning, middle and an end. You might want to mix things up a bit, however. The writer also has to decide when to begin and end the writing. It could start when she left home, but that would mean giving a lot of irrelevant information. This is a descriptive piece and the writer has decided that there is nothing worth describing before the departure from the first railway station or after the arrival at the second one.

The words and phrases in the 'senses' plan have been numbered to fit into the paragraph plan below. (This is more of an 'order plan' as some of the numbered sections would take up more than one paragraph.)

---

1. The city: railway station → reason for journey
2. The train: settling in on the train → people
    → foreign language
3. Through the window: city, industry, suburbs
4. The lady opposite: her story → sharing lunch → food
5. Arrival: being met at the village station.

You might prefer to order your description in a different way. Think about how you might rearrange the essay to create a strong and / or unusual impression on the reader.

Note that the focus of the description is the world experienced through the writer's senses. It is personal writing in which the writer's feelings (a 'sixth' sense) could also feature.

Exam Preparation

For one of the questions on page 86, try doing a plan based on the senses, including 'my feelings' as a 'sixth' sense. Decide how you would organise your answer and create a paragraph (or 'order') plan.

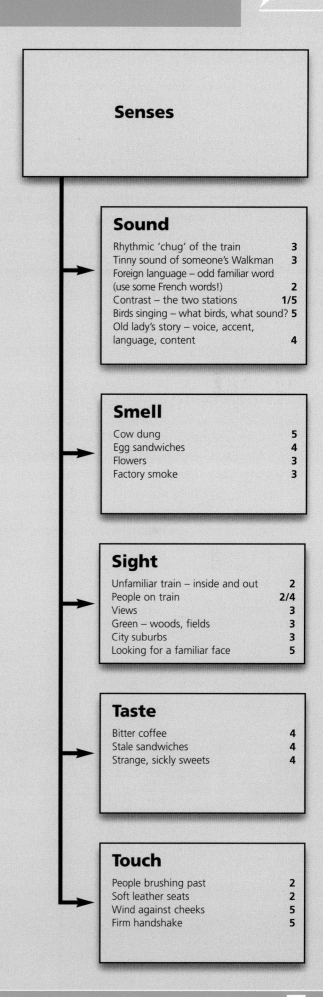

Senses

Sound

Rhythmic 'chug' of the train	3
Tinny sound of someone's Walkman	3
Foreign language – odd familiar word (use some French words!)	2
Contrast – the two stations	1/5
Birds singing – what birds, what sound?	5
Old lady's story – voice, accent, language, content	4

Smell

Cow dung	5
Egg sandwiches	4
Flowers	3
Factory smoke	3

Sight

Unfamiliar train – inside and out	2
People on train	2/4
Views	3
Green – woods, fields	3
City suburbs	3
Looking for a familiar face	5

Taste

Bitter coffee	4
Stale sandwiches	4
Strange, sickly sweets	4

Touch

People brushing past	2
Soft leather seats	2
Wind against cheeks	5
Firm handshake	5

Choosing Your Subject

What should you write about?

Where possible, write about something that interests, excites or amuses you: something that inspires you to write well. As with answers to inform and explain questions, this will probably mean writing about what you know. If it is something not many other candidates will know about, all the better – there are few experiences more depressing for an examiner than reading scores of descriptions of Disneyland (except possibly reading about people's mothers!). If you choose a commonplace subject, you need an original angle. Whatever you decide to write about, do not be afraid to use your imagination or your sense of humour.

Using Personal and Impersonal Language

Sometimes the question will have the word 'you' in it, perhaps asking you to describe *your* experience or to describe a place or person that means a lot to *you*. In such cases, you should use the first person in your writing. Other questions will simply ask you to describe something or somebody. These can be answered in a personal or impersonal way, or a mixture of both. Compare these two descriptions:

> Lake Garda, Italy's largest, is a dazzling expanse of blue originally created by ice-age glaciation. The glorious surrounding scenery varies dramatically from the severe grandeur of its snow-capped mountains to the tranquil serenity of its sandy shores and seductive vine-covered hills.

> The sunset was stunning; a vibrant canvas created by a wayward impressionist. Beneath, a gentle breeze caressed the yielding waves. I watched, as through a kaleidoscope, as the sky transformed itself from blue to purple, then pink and orange. I don't know how long I was sitting there. The others were looking for me, I knew, but I was transfixed.

While both pieces describe beautiful places, they are very different in tone. The first is written in the third person, which makes it sound as if the writer is giving facts rather than opinions. There is no real sense of the writer as an individual. This is the kind of description that might be found in a travel guide, where the aim is for the readers to imagine themselves in the scene and the writer's personal feelings are irrelevant.

The second is written in the first person and the reader is very aware of the character and what the view means to him. Both would be good answers to a question asking for a description of a favourite place or a good holiday destination.

Writing about People

You may be asked to describe a person. It could be someone who has inspired you, someone you know well or perhaps a stranger who interests you. This sort of writing can be very personal, and your relationship with that person will form part of your answer.

- Be careful not to fall back on clichés, especially when writing about someone you love.
- Look for what is different or unusual in the person you are describing. People who write about their grandparents usually say that they are lovely, kind people. This may be true, but it is not very interesting.
- Think about why you like – or dislike – the person, and think about anything that might amuse or intrigue the reader.

Here is a brief description of a person:

> Jack had lived above the launderette for fifteen years. Gnarled and weather-beaten, he looked older than his sixty years: his skin sun-baked and blemished; his forehead grooved with deep furrows; his few remaining teeth black and crooked. People rarely saw his teeth, for he had few reasons to smile when they were around. His one companion was his terrier Barney, whom he loved. In return Barney offered unquestioning loyalty and apparent affection.

This description sketches a vivid picture of Jack in just a few lines, giving the reader information about three important aspects of him:

1. **Physical description:** 'gnarled and weather-beaten … skin sun-baked… teeth black and crooked.'
2. **Personality:** 'few reasons to smile', '… Barney, whom he loved.'
3. **Background:** 'had lived above the launderette for fifteen years.'

When planning to write about a person you could start by considering physical description:
- What does he / she look like – hair, eyes, face, size?
- What does he / she like to wear?
- How does he / she move?
- What does he / she sound like?
- Does he / she have a distinctive smell?

Then you could move on to aspects of personality and background:
- What sort of temperament does he / she have?
- What are his / her beliefs?
- Does he / she have any special interests?
- Where does he / she come from?
- What is his / her family like?

Finally, you could think about your relationship with this person and how you feel about him / her.

Exam Preparation

Try planning an answer to this question.
Q. Describe a person whom you have never met, but admire. **Explain** why you admire him / her.

Writing to Describe

A 'writing to describe' question gives you the chance to show that you have a wide vocabulary and can use it in a creative way. You need to impress the examiner with your wide vocabulary, but remember that long words do not necessarily mean better words. What matters is the exact meaning you are trying to convey and sometimes the simplest words can be the best.

Techniques in Writing to Describe

- **Adjectives** are a basic tool of descriptive writing, so you will obviously need to use them. When choosing an adjective, consider whether it adds to the precision of your description and whether it carries certain connotations that will enhance your description. You could try using two or three adjectives together, e.g. 'a neglected, crumbling mansion'.
- **Nouns** should be chosen carefully, e.g. is your house a mansion, a bungalow or a townhouse? If readers know what sort of house it is they can picture it more clearly. These words also come with connotations, as readers might make assumptions based on prior experience about the sort of people who live in each kind of house.
- **Adverbs** and **adverbial phrases** describe verbs, telling us how something is done, e.g. 'the birds were singing joyfully'. Look for precise meaning and connotations.
- **Imagery:** the use of language to create images for the reader. Try using **metaphors** and **similes** to make your descriptions more vivid and individual.
- **Personification:** the use of a metaphor to give human feelings or qualities to an inanimate object or to an idea or concept, e.g. 'the house struggled for air'.
- **Alliteration,** used subtly, can have an impact. Think about what associations different sounds might have. A string of words beginning with 's', for example (**sibilance**), can create the idea of something slippery or sinister. Words beginning with a hard 'c' or 'k' can give an impression of harshness and violence, e.g. 'he clasped the crag with crooked hands'. 'P' and 'b' sounds give an impression of quick, explosive movement, e.g. 'Pete was pipped at the post'.
- **Assonance** works in a similar way, but it is the vowel sounds within words that are repeated, e.g. 'sweet dreams' or 'gloomy blue rooms'.

- **Onomatopoeia:** the use of words that make the sound of the thing being described, e.g. 'the crackle of leaves underfoot' or 'the steady chug chug of the train'. It can be effectively combined with alliteration or assonance.
- **Repetition** can emphasise an idea and give shape and pattern to your work, perhaps by starting a series of sentences with the same word, e.g. 'Darkness enveloped the street. Darkness seemed to cover the whole world that night. It was the darkness, not the cold, that made me shiver'.
- **Sentence structure / length:** long, compound sentences are excellent for detailed descriptions that draw the reader in and short sentences are good for impact. Try to mix them.
- **Voice:** use both active (e.g. 'lush green fields surround the house') and passive (e.g. 'the house is surrounded by lush green fields') voices to produce variation in your description, and make it more captivating.
- **Parallel phrasing:** phrases constructed in the same way and arranged in pairs or sequences can be very effective, e.g. 'the pavements shone with snow; the windows glittered with frost; and my heart was filled with hope'.
- **Fragments** are very good for impact and emphasis in descriptive writing, e.g. 'the sunset was a rainbow of colour. Simply beautiful'.
- **Ellipsis** can be used to show suspense and anticipation.
- **Present tense** makes the events described seem more alive and involving.
- **First person personal pronoun:** writing from a personal view draws the reader in.

Examiner's Tips

Try to think of your own, original similes and metaphors, rather than relying on ones you have heard / read before. Some are so commonplace that they have become clichés (e.g. 'sleeping like a log'). Try to avoid overdone phrases: the examiners want to see originality in your answer. Thinking up your own will be much more effective.

A well-placed rhetorical question or list of three, if not overdone, can help to lift a descriptive piece.

Look at the following short example of writing to describe. It is a vivid description of what is thought to be an ancient monument or burial ground.

(In the exam you will be expected to write more than this.)

This descriptive piece of writing uses a combination of short sentences and long sentences to create effect. It uses both the active and the passive voice, and employs a range of effective adjectives, adverbs, nouns and verbs.

Exam Preparation

Rewrite the following description, using some of the techniques given here to make it clearer and more vivid for the reader:

> I turned the corner into the street. I could see a lot of buildings around me. It was dark but there was a moon. There were people walking up and down the street and standing in doorways. A dog barked at me. I was frightened. I started to run.

Passive voice

Metaphor

Simile, rhetorical question and rule of three

Personification

Alliteration / sibilance

First person

Fragments

Present tense

Repetition

Lists of adjectives

Ellipsis

Imagery

It is cold. Yet the sun blazes golden, cradled in a hard blue sky. Silence. To the right a neat, rounded, still verdant hill thrusts confidently towards that star. Its regularity suggests something shaped by man. But which men? Who were these ancients who laboured, without machinery, to create something as pleasing to the mathematician's eye as the great cathedral domes of London, Florence and Rome? Perhaps it was carved from nature to praise their god and bear witness to his power, or perhaps its purpose was more sinister: an act of aggression or of desperation, built to defend the last remnants of their long-buried civilisation.

Strangely, the snow has not touched this hill. Its neighbour, to our left, has not been spared. The irregular contours of this sleeping giant are draped in a soft cloak of virgin white. Pure, yet seductive, its soft outlines invite us. We do not resist. As we start our climb, the only sound is of boots breaking the morning snowfall. If we stop, the silence is unbroken. The wind stings and caresses in turn. A solitary kestrel swoops, smoothly cutting the air, following a prey seen only by itself. Suddenly there are voices, and we realise we are not alone here...

To our left, making their way slowly up a snowy trail, is a young couple. Full of energy, vim and vigour, they playfully chase each other, stopping momentarily to steal a brief embrace.

The serenity of the hills is broken, but their impressive majesty remains.

Exam Tips

Useful Words and Phrases

You need to show that you can link your ideas effectively, whether within sentences, between sentences or between paragraphs. Words and phrases that link ideas or events are called connectives or discourse markers. A and A* candidates integrate them subtly into their work so that the answers are fluent and pleasurable to read. Here are some examples of words and phrases that could be useful as discourse markers in writing to inform, explain or describe (see also page 35):

- **To add information or build on ideas:**
  In addition, As well as, Furthermore, Moreover, Similarly, In the same way
- **To introduce a contrasting idea or point of view:**
  Nevertheless, On the other hand, Despite, In spite of, In contrast, Whereas, Rather than
- **To express cause and effect:**
  As a result, Therefore, Consequently, In order to, Inevitably
- **To give order to your ideas:**
  Firstly, Finally, In conclusion, Overall, Essentially, In summary
- **To express passing time:**
  Subsequently, Later, Before this, Previously, Immediately, The following day / night / week / year etc., As soon as, Meanwhile, During

Checking Your Work

You have 45 minutes to write your answer. Of this you should spend five minutes planning your answer and five minutes checking your work. Even if you feel quite confident about spelling, punctuation and grammar, it is easy to make careless errors under pressure. Make sure you have…

- written in clear paragraphs, which are linked effectively
- used a variety of sentence structures appropriately
- correctly used a variety of punctuation, including full stops, commas, apostrophes and (if appropriate) question marks, dashes, colons and semi-colons
- spelt words correctly
- crossed out mistakes neatly and written in corrections clearly.

If you make mistakes with simple words or straightforward punctuation, your work cannot be given a good grade. However, if you are trying to be adventurous with your choice of vocabulary and sentence structure, you may be forgiven for making the odd error.

Index

A

Accent 6, 50
Active voice 36, 78
Address 16, 20
Adjectival phrases 21
Adjectives 50, 92, 93
Adverbs 50, 92, 93
Advise 29
Alliteration 6, 16, 39, 50, 92, 93
Ambiguity 6, 50
Anecdotes 18, 83
Antiphrasis 79
Apostrophe 4
Argue 29, 40, 41
Articles 24, 37, 80
Assonance 6, 50, 92
Audience 15, 31, 75, 87
Autobiography 11, 21

B

Big to small technique 88
Biography 11, 23
Blessing 54, 67, 68, 70, 71
Bold 18, 22
Broadsheet 14
By-line 14

C

Caption 14
Checking 8, 46, 94
Colon 4
Colour 18, 22
Columns 14
Comma 4
Conditional sentences 33, 42, 43, 44, 45, 84, 85
Connectives 35, 40, 41, 42, 43, 44, 45, 46, 84, 85, 94
Connotations 6, 16, 50
Content 50
Contrast 6, 39, 50
Cross-heads 14
Culture 49

D

Dash 4
Describe 73
Description 17
Dialect 6, 50
Dialogue 50
Diary 25
Discursive essays 82

E

Editorial 14
Elision 6, 50
Ellipsis 4, 92, 93

E (cont.)

Emotive language 16, 39
Enjambment 6, 50
Exaggeration 16, 40, 42, 43
Exam question 8, 10, 28, 48, 69, 72
Exam tips 8, 27, 46, 69
Exclamations 6, 18, 33, 40, 41, 44, 45, 50
Explain 73, 84, 85

F

Fact 19, 20
Feature article 14
Figures of speech 17
FLAP 31
Font size 14, 22
Font style 18
Font type 14, 18, 22
Form 15, 22, 31, 37, 39, 75, 80, 82, 87
Formal register 75
Fragment 21, 77, 92, 93
Full stop 4

G

Grammar 5, 31

H

Half-Caste 61, 67, 68
Headline 14, 18, 22, 37, 80
Human interest story 14
Humour 79
Hurricane Hits England 66, 68
Hyperbole 16

I

Illustrations 18
Imagery 6, 17, 50, 92, 93
Images 18, 22
Imperatives 18, 33, 44, 45, 78
Impersonal writing 83, 90
Indentation 50
Infinitives 36, 40, 41, 84, 85
Inform 73, 84, 85
Informal register 75
Interrogatives 6
Irony 6, 50, 79
Island Man 53, 68
Italic 14, 18, 22

J

Jargon 15
Juxtaposition 6, 16, 50, 79

K

Key words 12

Index

L

Language 15, 31, 75
Language techniques 31, 40, 41, 42, 43, 44, 45, 84, 85, 92, 93
Language terms 50
Layout 22
Lead story 14
Leaflets 38, 82
Letters 81
Limbo 51, 68
Lineation 6, 50
Lists 39, 84, 85
Litotes 79
Logo 14, 18, 22
Love After Love 62, 68
Lower case 18, 22

M

Media text 11, 21, 24, 26, 27
Meiosis 79
Metaphor 6, 17, 40, 41, 50
Modal verbs 5, 36, 44, 45, 84, 85

N

Narrative 15, 16, 20
Night of the Scorpion 56, 67, 68, 70, 71
Non-fiction text 11, 21, 23, 25
Not My Business 64, 68
Nothing's Changed 52, 67, 68
Nouns 92, 93

O

Onomatopoeia 6, 50, 92
Opinion 19, 20
Opposites 39
Oxymoron 6, 50

P

Paragraphs 34
Parallel phrasing 78, 92, 93
Parallelism 39
Passive voice 36, 78, 84, 85
Pathetic fallacy 6, 50
PEE 13, 48
People (writing about) 91
Person 20
Personal pronouns 39, 40, 41, 42, 43, 44, 45
Personal writing 83, 90
Personification 6, 50, 92, 93
Perspective 50
Persuade 29, 42, 43
Planning 8, 32, 76, 88, 89
Poetry terms 50
Presentation 15, 18, 22
Presents from My Aunts... 65, 68
Pun 6, 50, 79
Punctuation 4, 5, 31
Purpose 15, 20, 30, 74, 86

Q

Question mark 4
Questions 6, 18, 33, 44, 45

R

Received Pronunciation 7, 50
Repetition 7, 16, 39, 42, 43, 44, 45, 50, 92, 93
Rhetorical questions 7, 16, 39, 40, 41, 42, 43, 50
Rhyme 7, 50
Rhythm 7, 50
Rule of three 16, 39, 40, 41, 42, 43, 84, 85

S

Sarcasm 6, 50, 79
Search for My Tongue 59, 68
Semi-colon 4
Sensational language 16, 39
Senses 89
Sentence length 18, 92, 93
Sentences 20, 33, 77
Setting 50
Sibilance 7, 50
Simile 7, 17, 50
Slogan 14, 18, 22
Speech 16, 37
Speech writing 39
Spelling 5
Standard English 7, 50
Statements 33
Strapline 14, 80
Structure 18, 20
Style 15, 31, 50
Sub-headings 14, 18, 22, 37, 80
Superlatives 7, 16, 39
Symbolism 7, 50
Synonym 7

T

Tabloid 14
Tenses 20, 78
Themes 50, 68
This Room 63, 67, 68
Titles 18, 22
Tone 7, 15, 20, 50
Traditions 49
Two Scavengers in a Truck... 55, 68

U

Underlining 18, 22
Unrelated Incidents 60, 67, 68
Upper case 18, 22

V

Verbs 36
Vultures 57

W

What Were They Like? 58